8

Never Call Me Mummy Again

PETER KILBY
with JANE SMITH

PENGUIN BOOKS

Peng   USA
Penguin Gro   nada M4P 2Y3

Penguin Ir   Books Ltd)
P

Penguin Books India Pvt Ltd, 11 Community Centre,
Panchsheel Park, New Delhi – 110 017, India

Penguin Group (NZ), 67 Apollo Drive, Rosedale, Auckland 0632, New Zealand
(a division of Pearson New Zealand Ltd)
Penguin Books (South Africa) (Pty) Ltd, Block D, Rosebank Office Park, 181 Jan Smuts Avenue,
Parktown North, Gauteng 2193, South Africa

Penguin Books Ltd, Registered Offices: 80 Strand, London WC2R ORL, England

www.penguin.com

First published 2013

002

Copyright © Peter Kilby, 2013

Typeset in 13.5/15.8 Garamond MT Std by Palimpsest Book Production Ltd, Falkirk, Stirlingshire

Printed in Great Britain by Clays Ltd, St Ives plc

ISBN: 978-1-405-90929-7

www.greenpenguin.co.uk

I dedicate this book to my mother, who I never abandoned in my thoughts or dreams, and I thank her for the resolve and other aspects of my personality that I must have inherited from her that enabled me to survive until I married and began to live.

Acknowledgements

Thank you to Michelle, my daughter, who first set me on the difficult path towards writing my hidden history; to my wife, Anne, who helped me when I found it hard to put memories on to paper; and to Jane, who gently teased out my tangled library of memories and thoughts and made sense of them.

Chapter 1

The flowers that seemed to be hanging in a vertical bunch from an invisible vase on the small, polished-wood table were almost luminescent in the dimly lit room. My brother stopped a few feet away from where I was standing, hesitated for a moment and then closed his eyes. When he opened them again, he took a deep breath and stepped forward until his shoulder was almost touching mine. I turned my head to look directly at him and, as I did so, I realized my hands were sweating.

We looked down almost simultaneously into the open coffin and I could sense the same stiffening of my brother's muscles that I could feel in mine. At first, I didn't recognize the pale face that lay below us. It was the face of an old man whose pallid skin had an unnatural, almost waxen, texture. What struck me more than anything else, however, was how small he looked. I had always thought of him as big and very strong, but death had stripped him of the aura of powerful aggression he'd had in life, and by doing so it allowed me to see him for what he had really always been – nothing more than a belligerent bully.

I could feel an emotion rising up inside me. It seemed to be coming from the very centre of my being, from the place where, as a child, I'd imagined my soul might be. At first I couldn't identify the feeling that was spreading like liquid through every vein in my body. It certainly wasn't sadness: whatever else I might feel about the passing of the man who lay in the silk-lined wooden casket, I had no sense of loss or mourning.

When an involuntary sound like a suppressed cough escaped from my partially open lips, my brother looked quickly towards me and I immediately covered my mouth with my hand, like a guilty child. But it was too late to stop the roar of laughter from exploding out of me into the respectfully silent room. I'd had no warning that it was coming and once it started it wasn't something I could control.

I let my hand drop on to my brother's shoulder in a gesture of apology – or maybe because I felt an instinctive need to touch and align myself with another living being. And, as I did so, he began to laugh too.

'He looks so . . . insignificant, almost pathetic,' my brother said at last, the words fragmenting as he tried to catch his breath. 'Why, in God's name, were we so afraid of him?'

We were still laughing when we turned our backs

on our father and walked, side by side, out of the room.

Although it would be understandable if you thought otherwise after reading the last few paragraphs, I'm not a callous person. In fact I tend to be oversensitive to other people's misfortunes, and I'd gladly move heaven and earth to prevent the people I love from feeling pain or distress. If there's one thing that makes me believe there must be good in me, it's the knowledge that my wife, Anne, still loves me.

Anne is a gentle, kind woman and I know she couldn't love a man who hadn't earned her respect. For all these years I've held her love – and the love of my daughter – inside me like a precious talisman. Even when dark, unhappy thoughts of my childhood crowd in on me and threaten to swamp me, if I try hard enough, I can see the light that shines from their love and I can use it to guide myself back up to the surface again.

Every significant or momentous event in one's life is bound to elicit some sort of emotional response, and on that day when my brother and I stood looking at the mortal remains of our father in his coffin, laughter – born, I suppose, of relief – was the one emotion that came naturally to us. I had other complicated, confused feelings too, but my overwhelming sense was that some burden I'd been carrying since my childhood had been lifted off my shoulders as a result of my father's death.

I was a man when my father died. I was just two years old when I saw my mother for the last time. I remember very little about the day she was taken from the house on a stretcher, lifted carefully into the back of an ambulance and driven away. My only complete memory of that day – which is one of the most vivid memories of my early childhood – is of watching the ambulance as it backed up towards the front door. When it hit one of the wooden pillars that supported the porch, there was a thud and the whole structure began to sway precariously. I can remember seeing my father running to put a hand on the pillar, as if to hold the whole thing up. Then he shouted and banged on the side of the ambulance with his fist. If it hadn't been for all the panic about my mother, I don't know whether the ambulance driver would have escaped, as he did, without a bloody nose.

Of course, at the age of two, I didn't really understand what was happening – either when the porch swayed or when my mother was carried out of the house. The thought certainly didn't enter my head that she wouldn't ever be coming home again. I've always wished I *had* known what was going to happen that day, so I could have put my arms around my mother's neck and begged her not to go, although in reality I know she didn't have any choice and she didn't leave me because she wanted to, or because of anything I'd done.

My mother was twenty-eight when she died. The few memories I have of her and of the first two years of my life are vague, like faded, out-of-focus, sepia photographs. But I think she was good to me, and to my siblings too, from the little they told me about her over the years.

I don't think my father treated my mother very well, so perhaps dying was a sort of release for her – an escape from a life that may not have been a happy one. And maybe she'd have been glad to know that the child she tried to abort with a knitting needle – which was the act that led to her death – didn't survive either.

People say that children need their mothers. I certainly needed mine. I know there are many fathers raising children on their own and doing as good a job of it as any mother would do. But at the other end of the spectrum there are fathers like Harold E. Kilby.

I was born on 10 February 1942 – more or less slap bang in the middle of the Second World War. The venue of my first smacked bottom and affronted cry was a nursing home in a Cotswold market town. By the time I was born, my parents already had four children between the ages of three and eight; I was their second son. When I was a few days old, my mother took me home to a small, red-brick, three-bedroom bungalow in a village that was little more than a mile away.

The bungalow was next to an estate owned by a man called Colonel Howard and his wife, who everyone knew as Dr Margaret. For as long as I can remember, I've drawn comfort from the belief that my mother and Dr Margaret had a warm, friendly relationship: why else would someone who was a GP and local magistrate become godmother to the son of someone like my father?

If it *was* my mother who was responsible for creating the connection that existed between me and such a remarkable woman, I'm grateful to her, not least because it was Dr Margaret, with the help of my grandmother, who gave me my first insight into the way other people live their lives. It was a re-education that was to prove as enlightening as it was enduring, and I believe it played a significant part in opening my eyes to possibilities and options that changed and probably saved my life.

Most of what I now know about the time when I was looked after by my mother before she died, I learned many years later from my siblings. However, there are two things I've always known, instinctively and with certainty: that my mother loved me and that, whatever happened during those first two years, they were the best years of my entire childhood.

The fact that my mother died before I had a chance to be aware of and remember her, remains one of my greatest regrets. Although my father lived until I was an adult with a family of my own, it seems I didn't really know him either.

I never had any reason to like my father and there's nothing I could learn about him now that would change the way I've always felt about him. It wasn't until I was in my forties that I even considered the possibility that his character was anything but one dimensional, and I was very surprised to discover that he was quite a clever man. Before then, I don't think I'd given much thought to what he did to earn a living.

The experiences of my childhood had crushed any chance there might otherwise have been of having a relationship with my father; it certainly wasn't something he'd ever wanted to have with me. I'd never been interested in what he thought or what he did, because I already knew everything I needed to know about all the aspects of his character that impacted on my own life: he was nasty, brutal and self-serving and whether he was capable of caring about anyone – which I very much doubt –he'd never held any love in his hard heart for me.

In the 1980s, my eldest sister told me things about

him that made me wonder for the first time what sort of man he really was – or *had* been when he was young. When my sister was dying, I went to visit her several times in hospital and when I arrived to see her one day she handed me a pink business card and said, 'It was Dad's. I want you to keep it.'

She was sitting up in the bed supported by pillows and I knew she was nearing the end of her life. If she hadn't been so ill, I might have refused to take the card and told her I didn't want anything that was associated with or had belonged to my father. In the circumstances, however, that would have seemed cruel, particularly as it was obviously important to her. So I took the card and put it in my pocket, assuring my sister that I'd do as she wanted me to and hold on to it.

I'd forgotten all about it when I reached into the pocket of my jacket later that day for my car keys and felt the edge of it with my fingers. Pulling it out, I read the words that were printed on it:

Sets supplied, two shillings a week
Lissen Radio battery charging

H. E. KILBY
Radio Contractor

Established 18 years

My father wasn't much older than twenty when he married my mother, so I assume the business of hiring out radio sets and selling and repairing batteries had been started by my grandfather. According to my sister, our father – the H. E. Kilby whose name was engraved on the card – also added a new section to the shop where he sold what were called at the time gramophone records.

During those last days of her life when she was in hospital, my sister told me a lot of things I hadn't previously known. There were also some things she wouldn't talk about, including, for some reason, why our father either lost or had to give up the radio and battery business.

Three of the stories she told me gave me a particularly puzzling insight into a man I didn't recognize, a man who didn't sound anything like the father who'd plagued my miserable childhood and caused part of my soul to shrivel up and die before I was old enough to know that the way I was being treated wasn't normal. I sometimes wondered if he would have behaved differently if his mind hadn't been poisoned against me, although nothing could really have excused his cruelty and total lack of any paternal sense of being responsible for me and needing to protect me.

One of the incidents my sister told me about took place in 1937, the year that a silent film called

The Sheik was re-released worldwide. Even today, excitement is generated by all the trumpet blowing and media hype that accompany the release of blockbuster films. So it isn't difficult to imagine that at a time when very few people had televisions and when even radio sets weren't found in every household, a film starring the handsome Italian actor and 1920's heart throb Rudolph Valentino was a very big deal indeed.

My parents were living in a small town at the time of the film's re-release, and when the date was set for it to be shown at the local picture house, my father got permission to set up a stall in the foyer, bought as many records of the film's music as he could afford, dressed himself up in full Arab costume and sold his entire stock to eager filmgoers after each show. It was an astute and imaginative idea, thought up and put into action by a man who, certainly throughout my lifetime, never showed any sign of having either characteristic.

As well as being a good salesman, it seems that my father was also a clever engineer, as illustrated by another of the stories my sister told me. Apparently, when he was a young man he had a motorcycle with quite a large sidecar. One day, he fixed a control panel into the sidecar, lay down so that he could see out through a small Perspex window, covered himself with a blanket and drove the seemingly rider-less motorcycle around the town where he was living at the time. He was stopped eventually by the local policeman, who can't have been completely unsympathetic to my father's attempt to liven up the sleepy market town because he let him off with just a warning.

It's a story that paints a picture of a young man with a sense of humour and fun – as I say, a man I wouldn't ever have recognized as my father.

I've never wanted to feel connected in any way to the man I knew him to be, so it doesn't make me happy to think that I probably inherited my own practical abilities and interest in engineering from him. What makes me really sad, though, is the thought of how different everything might have been if he'd been influenced by a good woman rather than by the evil witch who became my step-mother.

The third of the most surprising stories was more in keeping with the man I knew.

When my mother was alive and we were living in the bungalow that was my first home, we had some chickens, a tortoise – which miraculously survived being run over by a lorry – and a red setter called David. I remember the chickens and the tortoise, but I don't remember the dog at all. It was really my mother's dog, but apparently my brother, sisters and I loved it passionately too.

'Within a week of Mum dying,' my sister told me just a few days before she died herself, 'Dad poisoned that dog with cyanide. I won't ever forget the sound of its screams.'

'That's terrible,' I said. I could feel tears welling up in my eyes. 'Why would anyone do something like that? Why was he such a cruel man?'

My sister just shrugged her shoulders and refused to talk any more about our father, and after she died, there weren't many other people who were able – or willing – to fill in any of the many gaps in my memory of my childhood. In fact, it was only relatively recently that someone filled in a gap I almost wish had been left unfilled and told me what my mother had been attempting to do when she inflicted on herself the injury that resulted in her death: it seems that it wasn't the first time she'd tried to give herself an abortion with a knitting needle.

Surprisingly perhaps, in view of the second horrible turn of events that occurred within weeks of the ambulance coming for my mother on that spring morning in March 1944 – less than a month after my second birthday – I consider myself lucky to have been born. I don't feel angry with her for leaving us unprotected and defenceless against the evil that came to reside in our house when she was gone. She must have been at the end of her tether to do what she did; I can't bear to think about how miserable and lonely she must have felt.

I have just one clear, precious memory of my mother: I was sitting on her lap while she fed me what I think was bacon fat. (It was a different era, before people were burdened by knowledge about the potential health hazards of the things they ate – and smoked.) As well as that one memory, I have one photograph of her, which shows a slim, pretty, dark-haired young woman with kind eyes and a shy, tentative smile.

It's funny how things that are locked away in your mind sometimes find a means of expressing themselves without your understanding what's happening. That photograph is a case in point: I didn't realize for many years that it was the reason why I collected, almost compulsively, porcelain figurines of slim young women with dark hair. I think I've been searching for my mother since I was two years old.

Chapter 2

We continued to live in the bungalow after my mother died, and although I can no longer remember many of the events that occurred there, I remember the house and its surroundings with total clarity.

Seventy years ago, we lived in a bungalow near the Cotswold Hills, in a tiny picturesque hamlet, which remains pretty much unchanged today. At the foot of a nearby hill, there's a sloping field bordered by a curve of woodland about a mile long and half a mile wide in some places. Nestled in a hollow beneath the escarpment that skirts the road is the bungalow where we lived. The estate adjacent to our bungalow, which was owned by Colonel Howard and Dr Margaret, comprised extensive gardens surrounding an imposing Victorian villa. On the other side of the villa was a large apple orchard, and beyond that a smaller area of soft-fruit bushes. Along one edge of a lovingly tended flower garden were some brick potting sheds with red-tiled roofs, and in the middle was a wooden summerhouse flanked on each of two sides by a square ornamental pond.

The estate boasted a green, hard-based tennis court, a cottage where the Howards' visitors used to stay, and a row of four smaller dwellings that were lived in by their gardener and other domestic staff. There was also a farm, which was situated beside a sharp bend in the road opposite the imposing wrought-iron gates at the end of the driveway leading up to the main house.

About fifty yards below the curved line of woodland at the foot of the hill were some farm outbuildings, which housed various animals, including two enormous hunters called Gazebo and Caesar, a donkey known as Honkton, and some goats and sheep. It seems odd after all these years, and after having forgotten so many things about my childhood, that I can remember those animals so clearly. I suppose it's because I spent so much time with them. I think I got to know them better than I knew most of the people who occupied the peripheries of my young life.

The bungalow had a kitchen with two windows – one on either side of the front door – which looked out on to a strip of yellow-coloured gravel. On one side of the gravelled area was a large wooden shed and inside the shed was a workbench on which my father had built a railway track for a magnificent steam engine. That steam engine would have been an object of fascination and wonder to any small boy, but I only ever caught glimpses of it when the door to the shed was left ajar, because I was forbidden to go inside.

Next to the shed were some grey stone steps leading up to a wooden gate, which was the rear entrance to the grounds of the big house. Further along the garden beyond the steps, and sunk into the earth, was a large circular tank, approximately six feet across and made of cast iron. A piece of terracotta pipe about a foot long protruded from the retaining wall of the garden above, and in the centre of the tank was what I can only describe as a slimy metal see-saw, except that instead of seats it had a bowl at one end, like the bowl of a spoon, and a heavy iron weight at the other.

In those days, before television and computer games, there was little in the way of audio or visual entertainment for children, apart from *Children's Hour*, which was broadcast on the radio on the BBC Home Service every day between 5 and 6 p.m. We didn't listen to *Children's Hour* in our house; we made our own entertainment, which, for one of my sisters and me, included sitting on the side of the tank watching and waiting for effluent from the big house to gush out of the pipe and into the bowl of the see-saw. We'd often sit there for hours waiting for the moment when the bowl was full enough to tip the scale and send the waste cascading into the tank and the iron weight flying past our heads. (As I say, it was a different era and people didn't pay much heed to many of the health-and-safety issues that today seem like simple common sense.)

Opposite our bungalow, on the other side of the wooden five-barred gate at the end of the track that led down to the road, was a small stone cottage. The woman who lived there with her two sons – who must have been about five and seven years old when my mother died – was a divorcée called Flossie, a short, stout woman with a dark complexion and thick black curly hair.

On the sloping field rising up from the left of the gate was a dairy and pig farm managed by a farmer called Bill Giles. When I visited Bill many years later, he told me something I hadn't previously known, which was that my father and Flossie had been having an affair for some months before my mother died. I wonder if Mum knew about it, and if that's at least part of the reason why she was so filled with despair at the thought of being pregnant yet again. I suppose I'll never know – and it's best not to dwell on things that can't be known.

'After your father had paid Flossie one of his visits,' the farmer told me, 'he'd walk across my field on his way home. Sometimes, he'd pick up a can of milk to take back with him – to avoid arousing your mother's suspicions, I suppose.'

Bill was an old man by that time and I could tell he was trying not to show in his face the distaste he clearly felt at the memory of my father's deceit. But I was glad he wasn't able to hide it completely, because it made me feel better to know that someone had been on my mother's side, even if she hadn't been aware of it at the time.

Bill told me something else that was interesting during our talk that day: apparently, Flossie hated dogs. Maybe that explained why my father had poisoned David the red setter before the lid had even been closed on my mother's coffin.

It wasn't long – within weeks, at most, after my mother's death – before Flossie and her two sons moved in to live with us in the bungalow. Her cottage was never used as a house again. After gradually falling into a state of disrepair, it was demolished some years later. If only expunging Flossie's influence on all our lives could have been as simple.

I don't think I'd been aware that there were children living across the road. I'd certainly never met Flossie before the day she moved into the bungalow and we became a dysfunctional, unhappy household of two adults and seven children, with a baby on the way.

I did wonder sometimes when I was older if the injury that resulted in my mother's death had occurred in exactly the way my father described it.

Whatever the truth about how she died, she was best out of it all.

Before my father's mistress moved in, my mother had been the only adult female I'd had any close contact with and, being just two years old, I suppose it was understandable that I called Flossie 'Mummy'. When she grabbed me roughly by the arm and started shouting into my face, I was so startled and terrified that when I tried to speak I just made a stuttering, sobbing noise. My breath seemed to have rolled itself up into a tight little ball and had stuck in my throat so that I was struggling to swallow it. I was still making little choking sounds when Flossie dragged me across the stone-flagged kitchen floor, opened the front door and pushed me down on to the gravel outside the house.

If I close my eyes, I can still see the short-sleeved, red-and-black dress she was wearing that day. Every time she wore it after that – or even if I just saw it hanging on the washing line outside the bungalow – I had the same sense of shocked fear I'd had when I noticed it for the first time. In fact, that dress featured in my nightmares for years.

I don't have any memory of ever having been frightened or physically harmed before the day Flossie moved in, so I was completely bemused by what she was doing. As I lay curled up on the ground whimpering like a whipped dog, she wiped her feet on my back and shouted at me, 'If you are too stupid to understand anything else, understand this: you are an imbecile and I am *not* your mummy. Do not dare call me Mum, Mummy or Mother ever again. Do you hear me, imbecile?'

I *didn't* understand, but for years I believed that I was the imbecile Flossie so often told me I was – although I was clever enough to grasp immediately the fact that she wasn't my mother. I don't think I'd ever thought she was: it was just a name to call the woman who had taken my mother's place – in our house and in my father's heart (I suppose), although never in my own.

Of course, it goes without saying that there's a vast number of good stepmothers and stepfathers who have excellent relationships with their stepchildren. But just as there are bad parents, there are bad step-parents – the stories of *Snow White* and *Cinderella* must have been prompted by someone's reality, although I didn't know either of the fairytales until some time later, when I finally understood what Flossie's relationship to me really was: she was my wicked stepmother.

Although Flossie hated every one of my mother's children, her most ardent and vicious dislike was reserved for me. As a two-year-old child, I don't think I could really have done anything specific to have earned her dislike, so I assume it was due to the fact that I was the youngest and therefore the most in need of the care she was absolutely determined not to give me. Before I was three years old, her daughter – my father's child – was born, and from that moment, anything my own brother and sisters didn't do for me wasn't done for me at all. You grow up quickly when you have to, although there are some thoughts and fears children lock away inside them which remain there for ever.

My only memories of my childhood are of being punished in various ways and of sleeping outside on the many occasions when I ran away. Except for a couple of specific incidents, I don't remember going to primary school at all – although clearly I did, because I can read and write and I'm actually quite good at arithmetic.

Many years later, when we were both adults, my eldest sister told me that Flossie had wanted to get rid of me. The idea obviously had many potential bene-fits from my stepmother's point of view, not least because it would mean that the way would then be clear for the cuckoo she deposited in our miserable nest. I was certainly the victim of a lot of mysterious accidents at around that time. Somehow though, I survived them all, including the occasion when some-one released the brake on my pram so that it rolled down the grassy slope from the bungalow, tipped over and deposited me in the path of some inquisitive and always hungry sows. Fortunately, the farmer heard my hysterical screams and came running to scoop me up out of danger's way.

That was one of the incidents Bill Giles told me about when I visited him all those years later. My brother and sisters had always remained very tight-lipped about it, as they did about the many other dangerous near misses that occurred when I was small.

On another occasion, I was playing in the garden when I heard the sound of the steam engine puffing and whistling around the track in the shed. Drawn like a moth to a flame, I wandered slowly round the side of the house and stood outside the shed trying to get a glimpse of the train through the partially open door. Unfortunately, the shed door wasn't open wide enough for me to see inside, so I edged a bit closer to it, glancing guiltily towards the windows of the bungalow as I did so.

From where I'd been playing in the garden, I'd heard my father calling to Flossie in the house a few minutes earlier, so I knew the shed was empty. I was afraid of my father, and I wasn't such an imbecile as to have forgotten that he'd forbidden me ever to set foot inside the shed. But my curiosity was like an invisible hand pushing me forward. Maybe I was too young to understand fully the relationship between cause and effect, although that shouldn't have been the case, because I'd been punished often enough – for misdemeanours both real and fabricated – to know what would happen if I was caught doing something my father or Flossie had told me not to do.

Despite what I'd learned from experience, however, the pull of the steam engine was more than I could resist. I shoved my hands into the pockets of my shorts and tried to look nonchalant as I stepped closer to the shed. Glancing back towards the house again, I couldn't see any sign of life at the windows or any other indication that someone might be watching me. So, slowly and carefully, I pushed open the wooden door until I could see the magnificent engine chugging its way around the track.

I was still standing on the threshold when the engineer's vice that had been balanced on top of the door fell on my head. I dropped to the ground like a stone and the heavy block of iron fell on top of me, crushing my arm under its weight and tearing open my skin like a knife.

Fortunately, the vice didn't kill me – although it could easily have done so. In fact, it didn't even knock me out. But it did make a gash in my head so deep that blood began to pour out of it and I screamed so loudly and with such obvious shocked terror that Dr Margaret came running down the steps from her garden. One of my sisters had run out of the bungalow when she'd heard my screams and Dr Margaret told her to go back inside quickly and fetch a bowl of warm water. Then my godmother picked me up, sat down on the stone steps and lay me across her lap so that she could bathe the cut on my head.

Eventually, when the blood had stopped flowing, she tied a bandage around my head, dried my tears with the lace-edged handkerchief she took from her pocket, and handed a coin to my sister, saying, 'Take your brother into the village and buy him – and yourself – an ice cream.'

I was still sniffing pathetically as I walked along the lane clutching my sister's hand. Whoever was beating the inside of my skull with a hammer continued to do so for several hours. But it was almost worth the pain – which returned intermittently as the cut healed – to have my first taste of ice cream and, even more importantly, to have sat for a few moments on the lap of a motherly woman while she soothed my distress with gentle hands.

There were only two possible reasons why my father would have balanced a heavy iron vice on top of the shed door that day. The only one that seems feasible – unless my own father wanted to kill me – was that he did it to frighten and punish me if I failed to take notice of his order to 'Keep out! Savvy?' Whatever the reason, it was a terrible thing for a father to have done to his child.

Many years later, my sister told me that as well as wanting to give me a treat to counter the horrible thing that had happened, Dr Margaret had wanted to get me out of the way so she could talk to my father and Flossie alone. I never found out what she said to them, but whatever it was, it must have been the reason why they didn't shout at me or beat me when I got home from the village with my sister, as they'd normally have done. Instead, they simply ignored me.

I suppose I was too young for my mind to be able to process and make sense of most of the bad things that occurred in my childhood, so it simply blocked them out, which would explain why I have no memory of any of the events that occurred during substantial periods of time. And because there's so much I can't remember, there's no time frame for the memories I *do* have, so I don't know how old I was when various things happened. Over the years, some recurring incidents have become compressed into just one or a few occurrences. For example, I know that I was often beaten with the brass poker from the fireplace for being 'naughty', although I can't remember more than a handful of specific reasons for that particular punishment.

Some things do stand out in my mind though, such as the day when I said something – I can't remember what – that made Flossie really angry.

Her face became the purple-red colour it used to turn when she was going to thrash me. This time, however, instead of reaching for the poker, she grabbed hold of my arm, dragged me across the floor to the kitchen table, picked up a spoon and began to force mustard into my mouth. My lips were burning and it felt as if the tender skin inside my mouth was on fire. I struggled and tried to get away, but Flossie held me easily while she tied a piece of cloth across my mouth and around my head and then pinned my arms to my sides in a vice-like grip so that I couldn't reach up my hand to tear it off my face.

I was choking and there were tears streaming from my eyes. When the swirling fog of panic had cleared just enough for me to think, I realized the only way I was going to be able to breathe was through my nose, and to do *that* I had to keep completely still. I can remember looking down at the dark, mottled skin of Flossie's muscular arms, which were wrapped tightly around my body, and feeling the fear suddenly ebbing away. She must have thought I was bluffing when I stopped kicking and struggling, because she didn't loosen her grip on me. She just laughed in the nasty, sneering way she always did when she knew she'd shown me unequivocally that she had the upper hand – as if that was ever in dispute!

I've always been slow to anger and have never felt real hatred for anyone except Flossie and my father. And it was hatred I felt that day, despite my young age. It was like something cold seeping into every part of my body. Although I couldn't do anything to stem the flow of my tears, I made a silent vow to myself that I would never again give Flossie the satisfaction of knowing she'd hurt me.

Even when my stepmother wasn't actively punishing me, she treated me roughly and unkindly. Her idea of the way to wash a small child – at least, her idea of how to wash *me*, as she didn't treat her own children in the same way – was to sit me on the wooden draining board in the kitchen, fill the chipped, white porcelain sink with cold water, and scrub me from head to toe with the brush she used to scrub the kitchen floor. When I shivered and whimpered and my skin became so red and sore that it bled, she'd slap the back of my head, swear at me and scrub even harder. Fortunately it was a time before it was considered normal to have a shower every day, so this painful ritual occurred only once a week, at most.

One of the ways in which I was often punished was to have my hands tied behind my back and a piece of cloth fastened tightly across my mouth before being locked in a room and left there for hours. On one occasion when I was a bit older, I kept twisting and turning my arms until I managed to free my hands from the rope. Terrified in case someone came to check on me – which, in fact, they rarely did – I slid a piece of paper under the door and found something to poke through the lock until I heard the dull thud of the key as it fell on to the floor outside.

I held my breath and listened, but no one came – perhaps I was alone in the house. After a moment, I began to pull the paper towards me, praying as I did so that the gap under the door was big enough for the key to pass through. Then I unlocked the door and fled to the woods to hide. Of course, I had to go home eventually and pay the price of having escaped, and the key was never again left in the door, but at least I knew what success felt like – even if it was a very small and ultimately self-defeating victory.

Despite the fact that the misery of my life at that time was almost unremitting, I do have a couple of pleasant memories of things that occurred while we were living in the bungalow. One image that stays with me is of picking wild strawberries in the woods above the house and laughing as I stuffed them into my mouth and then licked my juice-stained fingers. I can also remember messing about with my brother and sisters as we dragged an iron-wheeled trolley into the woods to collect kindling for the fire.

The good memories are fleeting, however, and

too insubstantial to hold much sway against the tide of fear and unhappiness that still threatens to engulf me whenever I think about my childhood. It seems that I was either completely ignored or in trouble, and it was years before I realized that I didn't often actually *do* anything wrong when I was a small child.

By the time I was about three and a half years old, Flossie had decided I didn't need shoes. I can see it must have been expensive to feed and clothe eight children – and if someone was going to have to do without in any situation, we didn't need to draw straws to find out who it was going to be. Although my feet were often so cold that the skin felt, paradoxically, as if it was burning, I soon learned that there was a significant advantage to having bare feet, particularly in comparison to the ill-fitting shoes I had to cram my feet into later when I started going to school. Barefooted, I was nimble and could run fast, and I *did* need to be fast on my feet on the many nights when my stepmother flew into a rage and chased me out of the bungalow. Screaming like a banshee, she'd try to grab hold of me so that she could give me a good beating before pushing me out of the door, and I'd run like a greyhound through the kitchen trying to get out of the house before she caught me.

Sometimes, I'd manage to tip up a stool as I ran, although that was actually a bit of a double-edged sword. Whereas stumbling over the obstacle I'd thrown in her way might slow Flossie down enough to give me the few extra seconds I needed to pull open the front door and sprint out into the night, if she *did* catch me after banging her ample shins on a stool, the beating she gave me was even more vicious than it might otherwise have been.

Looking back on it when I was older, I couldn't understand why no one except me was able to see the inherent injustice in the fact that bruising her leg while chasing me around the kitchen caused Flossie almost to froth at the mouth with rage, whereas I was supposed to stand there and let her beat me, without doing anything to try to protect myself.

What mattered most of all when Flossie was chasing me was getting out of the house before she caught me, because she rarely bothered to pursue me once I was outside. However fleet of foot I might have been, there were many occasions when she managed to grab a flailing arm or the edge of my shorts, and then I knew I was in really big trouble. Sometimes she beat me with the poker, and sometimes she half dragged, half carried me outside and dropped me into the big stone trough that stood at the edge of the gravel path that encircled the house. In the winter the water was icy cold and when she held my head under its surface until the blood was pounding in my ears, it felt as though my lungs had frozen solid and I wouldn't be able to breathe even when she pulled me out again.

After I'd (almost) perfected the art of not crying when I was being punished, I would grit my teeth and try not to make any sound at all when Flossie or my father hurt me, which only made their beatings more severe and Flossie's attempts to half drown me more prolonged. I often cried silently when I was alone in my bed, but I was determined not to give any outward sign of the physical – or emotional – pain I suffered at the hands of my stepmother and father. Eventually, the stubborn streak that had been created by their harsh treatment set like concrete inside me.

Despite my best attempts at bravado, there was one punishment – which was administered by my father – that always broke my resolve and made me cry out.

When I was still a very little boy, I often ran away from the bungalow and spent the night outside. I knew I'd be punished when I went home – which, of course, I always had to do in the end. But sometimes the prospect of being outside and alone in the dark was less frightening than remaining in the house that should have been the one place where I felt safe.

My running away made my father almost incandescent with rage. 'You won't be able to run away if you can't put your feet on the ground, you little bastard,' he'd shout at me as he held me across his knees tightly with one hand while he beat the soles of my feet with a piece of wood until they bled. As well as the psychological effects that might be expected to result from being viciously beaten by your own father, this had a damaging physical effect too, and I still can't stand for very long, and suffer excruciating pain in my feet whenever I walk uphill.

Sometimes when I ran away, the front door would be slammed behind me and I'd be locked out of the house and left to my own devices, and sometimes Flossie or my father *would* come looking for me. I quickly learned some tricks to help me avoid getting caught. For example, I knew that when I threw myself down on the ground among the ferns or in some other hiding place when I was being chased, it was the sound of my rapid breathing that gave me away. So, instead of puffing and panting noisily – as my pursuer would be doing – I'd open my mouth as wide as I could and take deep, slow, silent breaths.

There were many occasions when Flossie or my father was standing so close to where I was crouching that I could have reached out my hand and touched them. I never did, of course. I just hugged my knees to my chest, hoping they couldn't hear the thudding of my heart, which sounded very loud in my own ears. Then, when they'd moved on, I'd sit there a little while longer, smiling to myself and relishing the glow of triumph that warmed my body for a few moments like a hot drink does when you're cold.

There was little else to smile about in my life.

Chapter 3

By the time I was four years old, I was regularly spending nights outside, and I could have given Bear Grylls a run for his money in any den-making competition.

I made one den among the tall ferns. During the summer months, the ferns were green and flexible, but as the autumn approached, they started to turn brown and become brittle and many of them were crushed and broken by the weather or by the passage of animals. I was subjected to many steep learning curves and faced with many problems that had to be solved and I learned the hard way that the edges of the almost-square stems of ferns are razor sharp. Although they can be bent over relatively easily, breaking them or pulling them up out of the ground is quite another matter.

The first time I grabbed hold of the stem of a green fern and tried to yank it out of the soil, I ended up with four thin, bloody and very painful cuts on my hand. But I soon discovered that by bending them over and tying them to each other, I could make a shelter that would keep out most of the rain during even the heaviest of downpours and give me a place to hide when danger threatened.

In fact, rain made me feel safe – I still like it to this day – because, although Flossie and my father would sometimes chase me, they knew, as I did, that by running away I was only postponing my punishment. So I suppose they thought, why bother to venture out into a cold, wet night when all we have to do is sit at home in the warm and wait till he returns?

My other den was in the woods beyond the field that sloped up behind the house where Flossie used to live before she moved into our home and our lives. The woods were surrounded by a swathe of brambles, which was only broken by the little tracks made by the frequent passage of small animals. Because of the physical barrier provided by the brambles, I felt safer and more protected in the woods than I did among the ferns. Another advantage was that it was easier for me to move freely through the woods than over ground covered by dense, tangled roots and the tall, thick fronds of the ferns. However, when I was being chased, I usually had no choice about my hiding place, because the ferns were closer to the house and I always knew that my only real chance of not being caught was to hide as soon as I could.

I was proud of my dens. Flossie often told me

that I was an imbecile – it was a word I understood, by implication, from a very young age. But when I looked at the shelters I'd constructed all by myself, I'd believe – for a few moments at least – that she was wrong.

Looking back on that time now from the viewpoint of an adult, I think I was a brave little boy in many ways. I wasn't really afraid of the dark and I wasn't lonely when I was on my own. I suppose everything's relative, and the things that would normally frighten a child were actually less daunting and miserable for me than being at home with my nearest and dearest.

I say I wasn't afraid, but that isn't strictly true. Children can learn to live with almost anything: normal is whatever they're told it is because they don't know that someone else's normal might be any different. But no four-year-old child spends nights all alone crouched in a cobbled-together shelter in the dark without being scared, and I certainly sometimes cried and often held my breath and listened anxiously to some unidentifiable noise, hoping that whatever animal was making it didn't want to eat me.

On really bad nights, when the rain was torrential and a bitterly cold wind was forcing its way into every corner of my den, I'd sneak into one of the cowsheds on the farm. It was warmer in there than it was outside and I knew I didn't need to be afraid of the cows. They turned their heads slowly as I crept into their barn and watched me with their huge brown eyes in the semi-darkness as I fell asleep with the hot smell of animals and straw tickling my nostrils.

When I think about my life now and about the man I am today, I don't feel connected to the little boy whose childhood was damaged beyond repair by his father and stepmother. It's as if we're two completely separate, unrelated people, and I feel desperately sorry for the little boy I used to be. I'm overwhelmed by immense sadness when I imagine him all alone in one of those dens, crouching in the darkness of the night with his little stomach rumbling and his eyes growing heavier and heavier until he falls asleep with his head on his knees. No child should have to experience that. And no child should have to live in constant fear of the people who should be protecting and taking care of him – although I know that many do.

My brother and sisters rarely came to my defence when I was in trouble with Flossie or our father – which was most of the time unless I was being ignored. Although the apparent indifference of my own siblings hurt me at the time, I realized as I got older that I couldn't really blame them: when you live with people like our father and stepmother, you quickly learn the art of self-preservation – and if you aren't being punished yourself, why go looking for trouble?

The problem is that the adults in a family set the pattern for everyone's behaviour, and because Flossie and my father bullied me and were unkind to me, my siblings behaved towards me in the same way. I suppose a child's natural instinct is to align him- or herself with the strongest against the weakest – which, in our family, meant at least appearing to be on the side of our father and stepmother and against me.

The one thing my brother and sisters did sometimes do for me was leave food in one of several hiding places outside the bungalow when I'd been locked out at night. They were taking a big risk by doing it, because they'd have been thrashed if they'd been found out.

I was always hungry when I had to sleep outside, so when I was certain that my stepmother and father had given up searching for me – or hadn't even bothered to start doing so – I'd wait a bit longer and then sneak back to the house looking for food. Sometimes, there wasn't any and my heart would sink when I discovered that the last hiding place was empty, like all the others. When that happened, I'd go back to my den and gnaw on one of the mangels I'd picked up from the farmyard across the road from the bungalow.

Some people call mangels mangelwurzel or mangel beet; they're root vegetables that are grown primarily as stock feed for cattle and pigs, although they're sometimes eaten by people too, boiled, like potatoes or turnips, rather than raw as I ate them. In fact, they're surprisingly palatable even raw and I always had at least one hidden away in each den, and sometimes some cow-cake too, unless Flossie had discovered it in my pocket and shouted at me as she threw it away.

On the nights when no food had been left outside the house for me and I didn't have any mangels to chew on, my hunger would make me bold and I'd sneak silently into the kitchen in search of anything I could eat. I had to be very hungry indeed to take such a risk, however, because I knew that if I was caught, I'd be in worse trouble than even I could imagine. So I only ever did it on a handful of occasions, when the white noise of my hunger had blotted out every other thought from my mind.

The risk of getting caught would probably have been reduced if I'd waited until everyone had gone to bed and all the lights in the bungalow had been turned out, but by that time my father might have locked the front door. He didn't always lock up at night – people didn't in those days, particularly in the country, where burglaries from homes were relatively rare – but not being able to get into the house on a night when I was ravenously hungry would have felt like a disaster.

One night, led, like a donkey following a carrot, by the intense cold and the physical pain of my hunger, I crept back to the house before all the gaslights had been turned off. When I eased open the front door and stepped silently inside, I could hear the muffled sound of my stepmother and father talking in their bedroom. I held my breath and tiptoed on frozen feet towards the cast-iron, pot-bellied stove in the living room, which burned throughout the day and night during the coldest weeks of the winter.

I was standing beside the stove when my whole body suddenly began to shake, and I held out my hands towards the heat. I didn't hear Flossie tiptoe into the room behind me and before I'd even realized she was there, she'd grabbed my wrists in her own strong hands and pushed them down on to the top of the hot stove. The pain was so excruciating I think I might have fainted if my stepmother hadn't been holding me up. When I screamed and began to kick out wildly with my feet, she loosened her grip on my wrists. She'd probably only held my hands on the stove for a few seconds, but it was long enough to burn them badly, and I was sobbing when I turned and saw my father standing in the doorway of the living room. His face was clearly visible in the gaslight from the open bedroom door behind him and the expression on it as he looked at me was one of sneering, amused contempt.

In contrast to my father's indifference, Flossie was apologetic – which was something I had never, ever, known her to be before.

'Ah, I'm sorry,' she said, touching my shoulder and looking down at the red, already blistering palms of my hands. It was also the first time she'd ever touched me, except in anger. 'You took me by surprise,' she continued. 'I thought you were an intruder, sneaking into the house in the middle of the night. Come into the kitchen and we'll do something to make them better.'

Bemused by her sudden change of character and confused by the effects of shock and pain, I followed my stepmother into the kitchen.

'We have to draw out the burn,' Flossie told me, striking a match and bending down to light the gas oven as she spoke.

'Okay,' I sniffed, and when she reached again for my wrists I held out my hands willingly.

The heat from the oven transformed the intense pain into agony that almost made me pass out, and when I yelped and tried to struggle free of her grasp, Flossie threw back her head and roared with laughter. Then, abruptly, as if a switch had been flicked inside her brain, she stopped laughing and began to shout at me. It was something about teaching me a lesson and how I was an imbecile if I thought I could ever outsmart her, but I was too shocked to understand most of what she was saying. Thankfully, her tirade didn't last long before she bellowed at me, 'Get to bed!' and I stumbled out of the room, with all thoughts of never showing my emotions in front of her and my father forgotten.

I lay awake for a long time that night, crying silently into my pillow and trying to prevent the sheet touching the burnt skin of my hands, until at last I fell into a fitful, nightmare-filled sleep.

What I learned from that incident was that there are some things far worse than hunger. It wasn't until I was in my twenties, however, that I discovered heat can't 'draw out' a burn, which was something I realized Flossie must have known all along.

I don't remember how long it was before my hands healed, although I do remember holding them up in the wind trying to ease the pain. The good thing was that I was pretty much left alone for some time after that night, and I was given regular meals, many of which I ate outside on the porch. No one spoke directly to me – it was clear that my sisters and brother had been warned not to talk to me at all – and I soon gave up saying anything to *them*. In fact, being ignored wasn't a bad thing, because at least it meant that I didn't get into any trouble, so I didn't have to run away.

I didn't realize it at the time, but I suppose Flossie and my father were afraid that if I ran away before my hands had healed, someone might find out what had happened, and then they'd be in trouble. I'm sure, though, that if I had told anyone – and who would I have told? – my father would simply have claimed that I was a compulsive liar, and no one would have believed my word against his.

When I look back now at those days of my childhood, time is distorted: some periods have become compressed and others seem to have lasted for days or months when in reality they were probably quite brief. Even allowing for the elastic nature of retrospective time, I know it wasn't long before the slaps on the back of my head and the aggressive demands to 'Get out the effing way' escalated once again into beatings.

One of the things I got into trouble for a couple of times – before a few punishments helped me to remember what I'd been told – was talking to my half-sister. The little queen was her parents' pride and joy and I was told repeatedly – and soon unnecessarily – that I was not to go anywhere near her. Perhaps Flossie thought I'd give her the evil eye.

I was little more than a toddler myself when the baby was born and I had no reason to dislike the new addition to our miserably dysfunctional family. Clearly though, Flossie and my father thought otherwise, and if I went within even a few feet of her pram, my father would shout at me, 'Get away from her or I'll bloody kill you!'

When my half-sister was still just a little girl, she'd often go to great lengths to try to make me talk to her, but if I succumbed, I was thrashed for doing what I'd been told not to do. As you can probably imagine, the adoration – and inherited genes – of two people as unpleasant as Flossie and my father did the little queen no favours. Luckily, having been prevented from interacting with her when we were children, I had even less contact with her when I was old enough to choose the company I kept.

Although Flossie's most intense loathing was reserved for me – for whatever reason – she hated my brother and sisters too. But it was my father who I found it most difficult to understand, because he allowed her to punish us the way she did without ever standing up to her, even when her actions went way beyond anything he could have believed was defensible.

I was frightened of Flossie and I was frightened of my own father. Looking back on it now, I realize that as well as being a bully, he was a weak, spineless coward – as I suppose most bullies are – and he'd met his match in Flossie.

I found out many years later that when she was in her sixties Flossie went to see a psychiatrist and told him about the nightmares that haunted her sleep. Apparently, the psychiatrist said there was nothing he could do for her. I don't know why, although I'm pretty sure he didn't mean that she wasn't sick – anyone who knew anything about her at all could see that my stepmother's paranoid, self-aggrandizing, aggressive behaviour wasn't normal by any standard. I know how difficult it is to banish nightmares: because of what happened to me when I was a child, I had them for years, and sometimes still do. So it only seems fair that Flossie's nightmares continued too – hopefully, until the day she died.

It wasn't just me and my siblings who regularly drove Flossie into a state of apparently uncontrollable anger. She often had vicious rows with my father, rows that would have been terrifying for another adult to witness, let alone a child. And she shouted and swore at her own children, although they always came first out of all of us, even above my father.

When I ran away I think Flossie's feelings about it were ambivalent. On the one hand, I know she was glad when I wasn't in the house; but on the other hand, the fact that I'd escaped made her almost wild with fury. I suppose it was a control thing: *she* was going to be the one who decided what I did and when I did it. Or maybe she thought that someone might see me sleeping out in the countryside, notice the bruises on my body and start asking awkward questions. And I always had bruises on my body, because every time I ran away, I eventually had to go home again, and when I did, Flossie made sure I paid a heavy price for my hours of freedom.

It was my running away that resulted in Flossie thinking up one of the most brutal punishments she ever inflicted on me. My father usually stood by impassively – he certainly didn't ever intervene – when Flossie was venting her considerable spleen on me. On this occasion, however, he took an active part in my punishment, which is something I was never able to forgive him for.

I can't remember what I'd done this time; I just know I'd spent at least one night outside in one of my dens. When I returned to the bungalow, Flossie flew immediately into a spitting, swearing, arms-flailing rage. She hit me several times across the back of the head and then grabbed my left arm and held it so tightly I thought the bone was going to snap in two. As she dragged me across the floor and into the bedroom I shared with my brother and sisters, her fingernails were digging painfully into my skin, making little red marks that started to bleed. I was wriggling and squirming as I tried to put my feet on the ground so that I could stand up.

Suddenly, she turned her head and shouted over her shoulder to my father, 'Come in here and hold him. Hold the little bastard while I teach him a lesson.' As soon as my father came into the bedroom and had locked his arm around my neck, Flossie hurried out and then we heard the front door open.

I was four years old and I'd already accepted as normal many things that no child should ever be subjected to. Subconsciously at least, I knew – because of the way I was treated by my family – that I must be unlovable. But what happened on that day when Flossie returned from the garden shed changed something deep inside me and, for the first time in my life, I wasn't as certain as I'd always previously been that I wished my father liked me.

While my father held me still, Flossie hammered a long metal nail into the loose skin between the big and second toes on each of my feet. Then, standing back to admire her handiwork, she smiled and said, 'Well, that should stop you running away,' although her words were barely audible above the sound of my hysterical screams.

I was leaning against the wall, close to losing consciousness, by the time my sisters dared venture into the bedroom to try to comfort me, and then to distract me while my brother pulled out the nails.

The wounds on my feet took a long time to heal and, when they did, they left scars that remain to this day. As anyone who was abused as a child will be able to tell you, it isn't the physical scars that are responsible for the nightmares that wake you up night after night soaked in the cold sweat of dread.

It was a terrible, unforgivable thing to have done to anyone, let alone to a small boy, but it didn't stop me from running away, which, by that time, had become almost an obsession. In fact, it had the opposite effect, and I began to spend even more time outside. There was nothing to be afraid of outside my own home – or, at least, that's the way it seemed. I could run like the wind and climb like a monkey, and I could almost forget the realities of my life when I imagined I was an explorer or a soldier living alone in the jungle with nothing except my own wits to rely on to survive.

Flossie and my father never told anyone that I went missing on a regular basis. Perhaps they hoped that if I did it often enough, I'd eventually encounter some mishap that would prove fatal and then they'd be free of me for good.

Without having any real markers in time to divide up my childhood in my memory, I don't really know what happened when, although I'm pretty sure that it wasn't long after the wounds on my feet had become thick brown scabs that Dr Margaret told my father and Flossie to find somewhere else to live.

My sister told me many years later that Dr Margaret had wanted to adopt me, but my father had adamantly refused. I don't know if that's true. I couldn't bear to think about it at the time: imagining how different things might have been for me made me feel as though I was suffocating. What I find most difficult of all to understand is why, if Dr Margaret did want to adopt me, she then kicked my father out of the bungalow so that we moved away from the one place where she could have kept a watchful eye on what was going on.

Whatever the truth was, we did leave the bungalow. I have a very clear memory of sitting with one of my sisters in a removal van on a journey that seemed to last for hours. Eventually the van stopped outside what looked to me, at the age of four, like a very large house, although actually it was just a two-storey plus basement Victorian terraced house – in a suburban street in a town in Kent.

Maybe that move marked a new beginning for Flossie and my father. For me, however, it changed nothing except the location of my ill-treatment and of my miserable childhood.

I don't remember going to school when we lived in Kent, although I must have done, and I think it must have been a teacher who gave me the bar of chocolate that became the focus of one of the very few good memories I have of that time. Sweets and chocolate were rationed from July 1942 – when I was five months old – until 1949, when they were de-rationed, but only briefly, because demand for them was so great they had to be put back on coupons again and didn't become freely available until 1953. It went without saying that any sweets Flossie was able to buy with coupons she ate herself, or gave to her own two boys and the little queen – who was always in first place in any queue when treats were being handed out. Of course, I didn't get to stand in the queue at all, so I don't think I'd ever eaten chocolate until that day in Kent.

Having something that other members of my family would want wasn't a situation that had ever occurred before, but somehow I knew instinctively that if any of them – young or old – saw my bar of chocolate, they'd take it from me. So I went into the toilet to eat it. It was one of those occasions when the reality is even better than you'd imagined it would be, and that chocolate was the best thing I'd ever tasted.

I've said I have very few good memories of living in Kent, whereas, in fact, that's really the only one. The next thing I remember is something that occurred when we hadn't been living there very long. I woke up one morning and found, to my horror, that I'd wet the bed. It felt as though my whole body was damp and I was shivering with cold. Often when Flossie erupted into a violent rage, I didn't know what I'd done to make her so angry, but I knew instantly that morning that wetting my bed would make her apoplectic with fury.

Although I didn't have any conscious memory of my mother, I did have a picture of her in my mind and I'd often try to imagine what she'd do or say if she was there. As I lay in bed that morning, trying to think of something – anything – I could do that might mitigate Flossie's inevitable anger, I missed my mother so much it felt as if my chest was going to burst.

I didn't know how to wash things, and even if I had known, there would have been no way I'd have been able to wash and dry anything without Flossie noticing what I was doing. To make matters worse, when I slid out of bed and lifted the edge of the urine-soaked sheet, I found that the mattress underneath it was wet too.

Then the solution struck me: what I had to do was ignore the damp discomfort and stay in bed long enough for the sheet and mattress to dry out. It wasn't a great plan – not least because, despite the fact that Flossie was happy when I was out of the way, she was very unlikely to leave me alone to lie in bed all morning – but it was the only plan I had. So I crossed my fingers, pulled the blanket up to my chin and tried to position as much of my body as possible around the edge of the wet patch that covered a surprisingly large area of the bed.

It wasn't long before the bedroom door was flung open and Flossie was standing in the doorway, hands on hips, glaring down at me with an expression of unbridled dislike.

'What do you think you're doing, lying in bed like some little lord of the manor?' She spat the words across the room at me, and then, without waiting for an answer, strode over to the bed, pulled back the blanket, gripped my arm in her vice-like fingers and dragged me out on to the floor.

She saw the wet stain immediately of course, and her voice was vibrating with fury as she shouted, 'Why, you little . . .'

In one smooth movement, without finishing the sentence, she hauled me bodily across the room towards the open sash window, lifted me up by my arm and half pushed, half threw me out of it. I don't know whether she was so beside herself with rage that she'd forgotten we no longer lived in a bungalow, or whether she simply didn't care that the window of the first-floor bedroom was at least ten feet above the ground. A fall from that height could have broken every bone in my body, or even killed me – and then Flossie would have had some explaining to do.

She didn't deserve to be lucky, but perhaps, for some reason, I did. As I toppled out of that window on a sunny morning in Kent more than sixty years ago, my eldest sister was in the process of cleaning the rugs outside. It was one of her regular chores and she'd already dragged every rug out of the house and piled them all up on the paving stones beside the clothes line, where she'd hung one of them and was beating it with a wicker rug beater shaped like a Celtic knot. I landed almost dead centre on the stack of rugs. It wasn't a soft landing and it hurt a lot, but at least I hadn't landed on York stone or concrete or whatever the surface underneath the rugs was made of. I was bruised and I damaged my wrist so badly I couldn't use it for weeks afterwards. But, all things considered, I had a very lucky escape.

What kind of person throws a little boy out of a window – any window, let alone one on the first floor? I suppose the answer is: the same kind of person who nails a child's feet to the floor to stop him running away, puts mustard in his mouth, and beats him with a poker; the kind of person who has neither morality nor empathy, and who can't – or won't – control their temper.

It was while we were living in Kent that my brother took a risk on my behalf – which was one of only two occasions when I ever knew of him doing so. It was when I was being punished particularly severely for something – I can't remember what the punishment was or what I was supposed to have done. 'If you don't stop it, I'm going to tell the police,' my brother suddenly shouted at my father. And although I don't have many things to thank my brother for, I have to admit that it took a lot of courage to say anything at all. My father must have taken at least some notice, because I do remember there was a brief hiatus after that, as far as punishments were concerned.

My brother was five years older than me – old enough when our mother died and Flossie moved into our house to be able to keep out of her way. I don't remember him, or my sisters, ever being punished to the same degree I was, but none of us was treated well. I think my brother used to have nightmares later in his life, so perhaps he had a much harder time than I was aware of.

I managed some time ago to put a stop to the screaming that used to wake *me* up – or, at least, to most of it. I did it by using a technique I learned as a young child of saying over and over again to myself while I was asleep, 'It isn't really happening. You're all right. It's just a dream.'

After we'd been living in Kent for just a few months, something must have happened. I've often tried to think back to that time and remember what it was, but I can't. Even in the last few days of her life, when it was obvious that my sister wanted to unburden herself of some of the things she'd been holding inside for so many years, she refused to talk about whatever it was that resulted in my being taken away from the house in Kent and from the rest of the family.

Chapter 4

Some of the things I can remember about my child-hood are like the abruptly changing scenes of a film. For example, one minute I'm lying in bed in the house in Kent watching the patterns and shadows dancing on the ceiling above me, and the next min-ute I'm in South Wales, living with a very nice couple who own a shop. It's frustrating not being able to fill in the huge gaps, but maybe there are some things that are best kept locked away in one's subconscious mind: what you don't know can't hurt you – or, as in this case, can't hurt you again.

One of my most vivid memories of living in Wales is of the couple I was staying with giving me a toy sailing boat. It was a large wooden boat – or maybe it just seemed large to me – and it had brilliant-white sails and a red-painted hull. Although I don't remember ever sailing it on water, I do remember very clearly the feeling I had when I held it in my arms for the first time and the man told me it was mine. In fact, he had to tell me several times before I was able to understand that I was being given some-thing so magnificent. He probably thought I was a bit slow-witted; the truth was that, with the exception of the bar of chocolate, no one had ever given me *anything* before that day.

Another good memory of something else that had to be explained to me occurred in the couple's shop. I was standing beside the counter when the woman handed me a small paper bag and asked, 'Do you see that big sack?' She pointed towards a large, brown hessian sack in a corner and when I nodded my head warily, she said, 'Take this little bag over there and fill it with some lovely sugar.'

When I hesitated, she placed her hand on the small of my back, gave me a little push and said, 'Go on.' When I still didn't move, she laughed, lifted my chin with her thumb so that I was looking directly into her face and added, 'You look as though you've just lost a shilling and found sixpence. Go on, boy. It's all right.'

To say that I wasn't used to people giving me treats would be a massive understatement. What I *was* used to – or I had been until I learned better – was being offered something and then being sneered and shouted at for being stupid enough to think the offer was genuine.

This time, no one shrieked and hit me across the head or snatched the bag out of my hands as I filled it with sugar. And when the woman smiled at me and said, 'Take it outside, boy. Go and sit in the sunshine,' I ran out of the shop, sat on a large, sun-warmed rock and thought about nothing except sugar until I'd licked the last crystallized grains off my fingers.

I wish I could remember the names of the couple I spent those few weeks with in Wales. They were very good to me, and I'd like to be able to put names to their faces when I think about them now. In fact everyone there was kind to me and within a surprisingly short time I'd almost forgotten about Flossie and my father. Of course, they were still there in my head; it was just that I stopped looking over my shoulder all the time anticipating the next angry shriek or physical assault.

My only other vivid memory of that time was of being taken to the house of a couple whose little girl had recently died. I don't know if it was common practice for a child of just five or six years old to go on a visit like that; perhaps the couple who were taking care of me simply didn't have anyone to leave me with. I must have understood that it was a solemn occasion, because I can remember walking sedately down the winding village road holding the woman's hand, instead of bouncing along at her side chattering, which I'd taken to doing as my crushed spirit started to revive.

The door of the little terraced house was open when we arrived and, as we stepped into the narrow passageway, we were greeted by a grey-haired, sombre-looking woman who spoke in hushed tones. When she opened the door of a dimly lit room and I saw the wooden box resting at an angle against one wall, I had no idea what it was. If I had known, I would probably have turned away and not looked, so that I didn't have to see the dead girl lying inside it.

The little girl must have been about seven or eight years old. She had fair hair and was wearing a pink dress, white shoes and little white socks with lace round the tops. She looked as though she was asleep, except that there was something too still about the way she was lying with her eyes closed, like some pretty porcelain doll.

I didn't want to be standing in that dark, airless room, looking at the body of a dead little girl. But I wanted to do the right thing, both because I could sense it was important and because I didn't want the couple who were so good to me to be embarrassed or upset by anything I did. So I stood silently between the shopkeeper and his wife while they bowed their heads and murmured the words of a prayer. Then I walked with them out of the room, and took with me from that sad little house an image that has stayed with me ever since.

However hard I try, I can't remember anything else about the time I spent in Wales, except that I loved sitting in the shop listening to the sound of people's voices, which was more like singing than talking.

Then the scene changes abruptly again and the next thing I can remember is being in my paternal grandmother's flat in a house in Cheltenham.

It was the first time I'd ever met my grandmother. She shared her flat with a lovely young couple called Nigel and Delia, and it was while I was living with the three of them that I first became aware of what was involved in 'normal' parenting. As well as buying books for me, my grandmother bought me the first underpants and vests I'd ever worn, and Nigel and Delia bought me toys. I can still remember clearly a toy rabbit – which, for some reason long forgotten, I called Wilfred – and a little red-and-yellow metal tortoise, which had a rather untortoise-like handle at one end, which you squeezed to make it move across the floor.

They gave me something else too, something that was far more important and life changing than any toy – they gave me their time and their attention. I can still close my eyes and see the pattern of the rug on the living room floor where we used to sit in the evenings and at weekends playing games together.

One day, I expect we'll know precisely how the mind works, and when that time comes, I think we'll realize that there are some things we knew, intuitively, all along. For example, it seems to me to be common sense that if bad things happen to children over a prolonged period of time when they're very young, the effects – in one form or another – stay with them for ever. But then if something good happens – perhaps at a critical time or for a particular length of time – it's as if someone's thrown a life raft into a wild sea: it isn't within your reach all the time, but it bobs past you periodically and if you try hard enough, you can reach it and save yourself.

The time I spent in Wales and, more particularly, the time I spent with my grandmother, Nigel and Delia, provided me with a life raft that kept me afloat on several occasions later in my life when I might otherwise have drowned.

I'd learned from a very young age to hide my true feelings. When I was living with Flossie and my father, I never showed them when I was happy – which wasn't difficult, because it rarely occurred – and I tried never to let them know when I was upset or when I wanted to cry. Perhaps that's why the many laughter-filled memories I have of my time in Cheltenham are so important to me, even now.

Delia, Nigel and my grandmother never shouted at me or spoke to me unkindly. They always explained things to me in a way I could understand and they often asked me what I thought about something, which no one had ever done before. In fact, the way they treated me changed my understanding of normality completely.

I can only remember one occasion when I cried while I was living in Cheltenham. When I woke up one morning, it had snowed heavily in the night and, after my grandmother had wrapped me up in a coat, hat and gloves, Nigel and Delia ran out into the garden with me to make a snowman. Afterwards, when we went back into the flat to dry our damp, snowball-splattered clothes and get warm again, I kept looking out of the window at the snowman, and as the day wore on and the light started to fade, I begged for him to be brought inside.

'It's cold and he's all alone in the darkness,' I told Nigel solemnly. He laughed at first, but when he realized I really was distressed, he became serious too, as he explained that snowmen prefer to be in the snow. I'd spent enough nights outside on my own to know that doing so was only preferable to being inside with people who were nasty, whereas the people who lived in my grandmother's flat were nice. So I kept insisting, until eventually Nigel and Delia managed to scoop up the snowman in a more or less intact state and bring him into the kitchen, where he melted and Delia hugged me when I cried.

Another wonderful thing about living in Cheltenham was the fact that my grandmother had a dog. I'd always longed for a pet, but as my stepmother and father had plenty of children to bully and torment, they probably felt they had no need to bring animals into the house – which, all things considered, was just as well.

My grandmother's dog was a black-and-white sheepdog called Roy, who was, in my opinion, the cleverest dog in the entire world. Every morning, my grandmother would put a coin in his mouth and he'd cross the road, alone, from the flat to the newsagent, where he'd put his front feet up on the counter, drop the money, take the newspaper that was held out to him and carry it back across the road to the flat.

It's amazing to imagine all the other skills and abilities that might be fostered by kindness, encouragement and praise – in children as well as in dogs.

Again, I don't remember going to school in Cheltenham, but, as I was seven years old, I must have done so. My overriding memory of that time is related more to the way I felt than to specific events. I was part of a family, which is what I'd always wished for, although I don't think I thought about it in quite those terms then. What I *was* aware of was not feeling anxious all the time and not being afraid to let people know how I *did* feel. To all intents and purposes, the wary, nervous, sometimes very obstinate child I'd been when I left Kent had been transformed into a cheerful, mischievous – normal – seven-year-old boy. Unfortunately, nothing lasts for ever.

Perhaps it's true that what doesn't kill you makes you stronger. If so, I owe at least some of my resilience today to what happened next.

In the catalogue of my compressed memories, one minute I was playing cards with my grandmother and the next minute I was at the bus station in Royal Well Road in Cheltenham with Delia and Nigel. Nigel was holding a small suitcase and the three of us were standing side by side in silence – a fact that was unusual enough in itself to have been the cause of the anxiety that was making my stomach churn so that I felt sick, even if Delia hadn't been holding my hand a bit too tightly and smiling in a not very convincing, almost tearful, way whenever I looked up at her.

When a bus swept into the bus stop beside us, I saw a look pass between them, and I knew, immediately and instinctively, that my days with my grandmother were over.

Standing on the open deck at the back of the bus like a stocky, belligerent, hard-faced camp commander was Flossie. I glanced quickly at Delia, but this time she didn't even try to smile at me. She just wiped her cheeks with the back of her gloved hand and whispered to her husband, 'Oh Nigel, do something. She's awful.'

It was as if a switch had been flicked inside me, transforming me instantly from a little boy who lived in a happy home and did all the things normal little boys did, into Flossie's stepson – frightened and with a sinking, heavy feeling of dread, but at the same time acquiescent in the face of what he should have known all along was his inevitable fate.

When Delia dropped my hand to wipe her face, Nigel reached for my other one and for a moment we just stood there. Delia was crying, Nigel was squeezing my hand in his, and Flossie was standing on the platform at the back of the bus clutching the metal boarding pole with one of *her* hands while reaching out towards me with the other, shouting, 'Get on the bus. Take my 'and. Come on, take it, yer little tyke.'

When Nigel didn't move I felt a small flutter of hope, like excited butterflies in my stomach: perhaps, now he'd seen Flossie for himself, he was going to refuse to let me go. The butterflies began to flap their wings with increased vigour when Flossie bent down, snatched the suitcase from Nigel's hand and grabbed hold of my arm, and Nigel still didn't loosen his grip on me.

'Let go of him,' Flossie screeched at Nigel, apparently unaware of and certainly indifferent to all the embarrassed, quizzical faces that had turned to watch the unfolding of the extraordinary scene.

'This has got nothing to do with you, so mind your own bloody business.'

'Is the lad getting on or are you getting off?' The bus conductor's finger was hovering over the bell as he waited to let the driver know that it was safe to move away from the bus stop.

By this time, all the passengers on the bus were watching and one of them called out impatiently to Flossie, 'Make up your mind.'

It seemed like minutes, but must only have been for a second or two that I was suspended, almost comically, between Flossie's and Nigel's outstretched arms. Then Flossie gave one final tug and Nigel let go of my hand. Dragging me up on to the platform beside her, Flossie gave a yelp of triumph, and at the same moment the bus conductor rang the bell and the wheels of the bus began to turn.

Pushed roughly down on to a seat, I slid across it towards the window and Flossie lowered her un-wieldy bulk to sit beside me. When I turned my head to look back at the bus stop, I could see Delia and Nigel still standing there. Delia was crying and Nigel had his arm around her shoulders.

I never saw either of them again, and it was a long time before I had any further contact with my grand-mother. But at least I knew – from Delia's tears and from Nigel's obvious reluctance to let go of me – that they hadn't been the ones to instigate my abrupt departure from Cheltenham, although God knows why Flossie and my father wanted to have me back.

In the only other memory I have of that day, I got off the bus alone, which makes me wonder if perhaps it wasn't the same day after all, because I can't imagine where Flossie would have gone, but I don't remember what happened in the intervening period. When I was met by my father at a bus stop in a Gloucestershire village, it was pouring with rain and I was carrying a heavy suitcase containing the clothes and books my grandmother, Nigel and Delia had bought for me. My father didn't greet me when I stepped off the bus; he just snapped, 'Follow me,' then turned and strode away across the main road, leaving me to struggle along behind him as best I could, the suitcase banging painfully against my shins with every anxious, hurried step.

The fact that I'm a dyed-in-the-wool, written-in-stone optimist is a source of constant wonder to the only two people I'd ever told about my childhood before I wrote this book. It was certainly either innate optimism or a total inability to learn from experience that allowed me to think, when I saw my father standing at the bus stop, that perhaps he actually *wanted* me back. It only took a few seconds for me to realize this wasn't the case.

I was still doing an odd sort of limping run along the road behind him when he stopped so abruptly I almost collided with him. He shouted angrily, 'For Christ's sake! Give the bloody thing to me.' Then he snatched the suitcase out of my hands, turned and continued to stride down the road at the same fast pace.

It was a long walk – well, it was a walk for my father; I had to jog to try to keep up with him. And it was made even more miserable by the torrential rain that was was clearly a source of irritation to my father even though he was wearing a raincoat, which was a luxury I didn't have. I was soaking wet and exhausted by the time we arrived at Laburnum Cottage in a village that lies between two only very slightly larger villages not far from the River Severn.

I don't know how long I'd been away from the bosom of my loving family or when they'd moved from Kent back to the Cotswolds. It was long enough for my siblings and the little queen to have grown so much I barely recognized them. Clearly, however, it hadn't been long enough for them to have forgotten that they didn't like me, and the only one of them to say a feeble 'hello' to me was my eldest sister. The boys – including my own brother – merely glared at me in an unfriendly, antagonistic way.

Wales and Cheltenham were in the past and I was 'home'. It was a realization that made my heart sink into my sodden shoes.

Within days of arriving I started at the local

school. Once again, it didn't make enough of an impression on me to have created any lasting memories. In fact all I remember about being at any school at any time during those years is of standing on the wooden floor of a large room with a lot of other children throwing bean bags around a circle. Perhaps the details of what happened during all the well-ordered, well-organized hours of my education have simply slipped out of my mind – or been strong-armed out by the more robust, more impactful events that occurred at home.

I had jobs to do at home every evening, one of which was to clean everyone's shoes, whether they needed it or not. That meant ten pairs: Flossie's, my father's, my brother's, my three sisters', my two step-brothers', the little queen's and mine. I had to do a proper job, which, as well as buffing every single shoe until it shone like glass, included polishing the welts and instep of each one. When I'd finished, my father would carefully examine the twenty shoes, one by one, and cuff my head, hard, with the back of his hand if he found even the smallest imperfection.

My father's favoured way of making sure I took notice of what he was saying was to explain something to me in an aggressive, slowly articulated way, as if he was speaking to the imbecile he and Flossie always told me I was. Then he'd put his face right up close to mine, so that my nostrils were full of the stench of his rancid breath and little specks of his spit spotted my cheek, and he'd shout, three or four times, 'Savvy?'

I don't know what happened to make my father the way he was. He certainly didn't inherit his character from his mother – the grandmother I'd lived with for far too brief a period in Cheltenham. Whereas my father was aggressive and volatile, my grandmother was consistently gentle and kind – and about as different from him in every way as it was possible to be. It was one of my sisters who told me years later that my grandmother had been very well educated and that her own father and grandfather had been wealthy farmers in the Cotswolds. Apparently, she and my grandfather – who died young so I never met him – more or less disowned my father when he married my mother. I don't know why: all I really know about my mother is that she was Irish and little more than a girl when she married my father.

Whatever his background and life experiences, however, there was no excuse for the way my father behaved. Perhaps if his family had stuck by him, things might have turned out differently – for all of us; but everyone has a choice about what sort of adult they become, and my father chose to be a self-serving, vicious bully.

As well as shoe cleaning, my list of jobs also included weeding the vegetable patch and clearing out the small pond my father had made for Flossie in the front garden. One day at a weekend, after I'd cleaned the pond, I went into the field behind the house, where I found two small mushrooms.

The sad truth is that children have a need to be loved – or, failing that, at least to be liked – which is so strong that, however many times they get hurt and knocked back, they continue to want to please the significant adults in their lives. I suppose that's why I carried the mushrooms home carefully and gave them to Flossie. Even that was a risk, because you never knew how she'd react to anything. On this occasion, I was lucky, and she was clearly delighted.

'Go and find some more,' she told me. 'Pick as many as you can find and I'll cook them for your father's tea.'

I felt almost cheerful as I scuttled back outside and began to scour the field for more mushrooms. I spent a long time searching but didn't find a single one, and as the sun sank lower in the sky, my heart sank too, until eventually I gave up and trudged back to the house empty handed.

Flossie was standing at the kitchen sink when I went in through the back door. I'd just begun to explain how I'd searched and searched, when she picked up the two mushrooms I'd given her earlier and flung them at me. It took me so totally by surprise I didn't have time to turn my head away or raise my hands to cover my face, and the stalk of one of the mushrooms hit me squarely in the eye.

'Get out!' Flossie shouted at me. 'I should have known you wouldn't even be able to do something as simple as pick some mushrooms. Go on, get out, imbecile.'

As I darted out of the kitchen before her anger could explode into rage, I couldn't help believing that I *was* the imbecile she said I was – for showing her the two mushrooms in the first place, if not for failing to find any more.

We ate all our meals at a table in the living room, where I sat on a stool that was always positioned just a bit too far away for me to be able to reach anything on the table except my plate. I wouldn't have dared move the stool closer or stand up, and as no one ever took any notice if I asked for something to be passed to me, I often ate only what was already on my plate and went to bed hungry.

The little queen always sat opposite me at the table. I still wasn't allowed to talk to her or interact with her in any way, which wouldn't have been a hardship at all from my point of view if it hadn't been for the fact that she often followed me around when I got home from school. Sometimes she'd talk to me and sometimes she'd just stare at me silently, as if I was some sort of freak.

One teatime, I was sitting on my stool when she said something and, without thinking, I glanced across the table at her. I had absolutely no warning of the punch that hit me full in the face and sent me flying across the floor. I landed in a heap in the corner of the room, shocked and choking on the ball of air that had become stuck in my throat when my father's fist made contact with my jaw.

'Get up!' my father shouted at me, and as I struggled to my feet, I looked at the faces of all the members of my family who were sitting around the table and saw on each one of them an expression of either sneering contempt or open dislike.

I went to bed hungry that night, and for every meal afterwards I was made to sit away from the table and facing the wall.

Chapter 5

There wasn't a bedroom for me at the house that had become my new home, or any space for me in the bedrooms that were occupied by the other children, so I slept on an iron-framed bed on the upstairs landing. The mattress was thin and hard and full of little lumps. On top of it, instead of a sheet, there was a threadbare, sandy-coloured blanket, and another blanket that I slept under, which was made of grey wool and was a bit thicker and larger than the one that didn't quite cover the mattress.

One night when I went upstairs to bed, my mattress had disappeared. No one had said anything about it, although I wouldn't have expected an explanation because nothing was ever explained to me. I didn't dare ask what had happened or if I could have another one. I just spread the thin blanket over the broken bed springs, lay down on top of it, covered myself with the other blanket and went to sleep.

After that first night, I tried not to mind the fact that the other children smirked in a mean-spirited way every time they walked past my bed en route to their own bedrooms. I could be a stubborn child and

I was determined I wasn't going to let anyone see that I cared. So I ignored their whispered taunts and simply turned my back on them – very slowly, because turning over on the metal springs of an old bed requires cautious manoeuvring.

I'd been sleeping without a mattress for several nights when I woke up in a panic one night, thinking someone was trying to suffocate me. Even before I was fully awake I was repeating to myself my usual mantra – 'It's only a dream.' This time though, it wasn't a dream: someone really was holding a pillow over my face and however violently I struggled, there didn't seem to be anything I could do about it. I must have been sleeping on my side with my face turned upwards, and somehow I managed to twist my neck and press it into the blanket underneath me. For once, I was thankful that the material was thin and full of holes. When I managed to hook my fingers around the iron bedstead, I held on to it with all my strength, even when I was punched and pulled repeatedly.

Then, as suddenly as it had started, the tugging stopped and the pressure on the pillow covering my head was lifted. Panting and damp with sweat, I lay completely still for a while, certain it was a trick and that as soon as I moved it would start all over again. When I eventually turned over on to my back, my attacker had gone.

For a long time after that, I'd wake up repeatedly in the night and lie in bed listening to the creaking night-time sounds of the old house as it settled on its foundations. I was afraid to fall asleep again, but at least having to sleep without a mattress felt less like a hardship than it had previously done – if I'd had one that night, I might not have survived to tell the tale.

I always woke up when Flossie and my father went to bed, although I'd keep my eyes shut, lie completely still and make little noises that I hoped sounded like the even breathing of deep sleep. It was never a good idea to attract their attention at any time of the day or night, but I always felt particularly vulnerable when I was in bed.

It was a vulnerability that my brother and stepbrothers seemed to be aware of, because whenever Flossie and my father went out for the evening, they'd stand at the bottom of the stairs whispering just loudly enough for me to hear, 'The boot is coming to kill you, Peter. Look out! The boot is coming.' Despite not knowing who or what 'the boot' was supposed to be, my heart would thump and I'd have to clamp my hand over my mouth in a desperate attempt to stop little whimpering noises escaping from it.

At the weekends and after school, when the boys had finished their jobs around the house, they'd sometimes play in the fields behind it. I was never much interested in playing the sorts of games they liked, and I soon learned to hate football too. Normally, they wouldn't have dreamed of letting me join in with any of their games, but when they needed an extra player for football, they'd force me to play with them.

Standing round me in a circle, they'd sing over and over again, in whining voices presumably meant to sound like mine, 'I don't *want* to play football. I don't *want* to play football.' Then one of them would reach out a hand to push or prod me and the words they were chanting would change to, 'Okay, I *will* play football.' I almost always gave in at that point, because I imagined there would be worse to come if I still refused to play with them – although it seemed to me that all they wanted me to do was stand in the goal while they kicked the ball at me.

One day, my brother and the eldest of my two stepbrothers called a truce. 'We're sorry,' my brother told me. 'You don't have to play football if you don't want to. Here, have some of this.' He handed me a half-full bottle of Tizer and when I hesitated, thinking that he was going to snatch it back and punch me for being stupid enough to believe him, he nodded encouragingly and said, 'It's okay. Go on. You can have some.'

When I unscrewed the cap and lifted the Tizer bottle to my lips to take a swig, my brother and stepbrother could no longer contain their hilarity. Just as I was about to swallow some of the amber-coloured liquid, they burst out laughing.

'We pissed in it,' my brother managed to say at last. 'It's piss. You were about to drink our piss.'

What was even worse than knowing how close I'd come to drinking their urine was the fact that, despite all the evidence and experience to the contrary, I'd allowed myself to believe they'd wanted to be nice to me. I suppose if you really, really want something to be true, you're sometimes tempted to believe the unbelievable.

One way or another, our family must have been a source of interest to our neighbours in the village, some of whom became used to hearing my frantic knocks on their front doors when I was trying to escape a beating. Despite the fact that an alleyway separated the two houses, the elderly couple who lived next to us must have heard all the shouting and commotion that emanated from our house on a regular basis, so they probably had a good idea what Flossie and my father were like. Perhaps that's why they always let me in when I knocked on their door. They were quiet, kind people and never asked me any questions; they just smiled at me and talked about everyday things while I sat at their kitchen table and ate the piece of cake they always gave me. At least I had a refuge

I could go to sometimes – and I often needed a refuge.

There's nothing like having appalling neighbours to make you feel better about your own life, and in that respect Flossie and my father provided the people in the village with what could have been considered to be a public service. Flossie had a constant, child-like need to be the sole focus of everyone's attention, and it was in order to get attention from *someone* that she stormed out of the cottage one day in the middle of a screaming fight she was having with my father and threw herself down in the middle of the road.

Whenever Flossie and my father had a row, I was always frightened by their aggression and on that day I was embarrassed too, because I was sure that everyone must be laughing at Flossie – and, by implication, at all of us. I don't think Flossie was embarrassed at all though, and after lying in the road for a minute or two without eliciting any response from anyone, she got up, walked back into the house and continued the row she'd been having with my father as if there had been no hysterical, attention-seeking interlude at all.

It had been months since I'd last slept out in the open when I ran away from Laburnum Cottage for the first time. After I got home from school one day, the little queen kept following me around, whining like a petulant prima donna. I knew that if I talked to her, I'd get into trouble. I'd been ignoring her for quite some time before I eventually cracked and said 'Yes' in answer to some daft question she'd asked me. As soon as the word was out of my mouth, she ran off to find her mother.

Within seconds, Flossie came barging into the living room like an enraged prize-fighter. Trotting along behind her, and opening the hands that covered her face to look at me as she bawled, was the little queen.

I didn't even bother to open my mouth to try to explain what had happened; I knew I'd be wasting my time. I just gritted my teeth and kept perfectly still through the beating that followed, and then, when everyone's backs were turned, I ran away.

I'd made a good friend at school, a boy called David, and it was to his house on the banks of the River Severn that I went that evening. His mother opened the door when I rang the bell and she called up the stairs to David, who came bounding down them two at a time, in a way that would have resulted in a smack round the head if not a full-scale beating in my house.

David's mother just smiled and we followed her into the kitchen, where she gave us pieces of cake on little patterned plates and told us to take it upstairs to David's room. She must have thought I was a bit dim when I stood there with my mouth open in astonishment as she cut the cake and chatted cheerfully to us both in a way I'd never heard Flossie speak to anyone.

I waited until we were upstairs and had eaten our cake before I told David that I'd run away. As an avid reader of adventure stories, he was instantly full of ideas about where I could hide – some of them more realistic than others – and about what he could do to help me.

Later, when we went downstairs, David told his mother that I was going home and he was going to walk through the village with me. But instead of following the lane to the cottage, we took a circuitous route down to the banks of the river where his parents had an old summerhouse.

During the several days I stayed in that summerhouse, David brought me hunks of bread and cheese whenever he could, and although being alone for hours on end somewhere like that sounds a bit miserable and scary, it wasn't. Compared to being at home, it was pretty good. It was boring sometimes, but at least no one shouted at me or called me an imbecile or a stupid cab horse. And when David brought me food, he stayed for as long as he could and told me stories from the books he'd read. Then he'd say as he was leaving, 'You're very brave,' and he'd tell me I was just like some intrepid explorer he'd heard about, whose name I can no longer remember.

I had to leave the summerhouse when David's father found out what was going on, but I was determined not to go home. I decided I'd sleep in a hedgerow, where, if I could find one that was thick enough, I'd be well hidden and could keep reasonably dry if it rained. I thought it would be just like all the nights I'd slept outside when we lived in the bungalow. But it turned out that a hedgerow is rather a different proposition from a den or a cattle barn, and sleeping curled up in a ball among branches and brambles that tear at your clothes and scratch your skin every time you move is even less comfortable than it sounds.

Although there were no mangels to be found in the fields, I did find some hens' eggs, which are surprisingly palatable eaten raw – when you're hungry enough. I also found a shed at the end of one garden that had been left open and contained boxes of stored apples and vegetables.

My forays in search of food had to take place in the dark, because I didn't dare risk being seen in daylight. Even the darkness didn't provide me with complete protection, however, and at one point I came very close to getting caught because I made a noise that probably wouldn't have been heard by a person but was picked up by the sharp ears of a dog. My heart, which already felt as if it was vibrating in my chest with each rapid beat, almost stopped beating altogether when the dog began to bark. I dropped the apples I was holding, darted out of the shed and ran. All those times when I'd had to run like the wind through the ferns or woodland to escape from Flossie or my father when we lived in the bungalow had been good practice and I managed to get away without being seen, although not without getting my legs covered in scratches.

If anyone *had* seen me, they'd have been appalled: I looked like the feral child Mowgli must have looked before Disney tidied him up for the film. I was filthy. Dirt was mingled with dried blood from all the scratches and cuts on my arms and legs, my hair was caked in mud and full of bits of hedgerow, and I smelt terrible. I'd wet myself several times and my underwear and shorts were soaked in urine, as a result of which, painful blisters had begun to form around my waist. As well as being very dirty, I was hungry, tired and often frightened, so perhaps I would eventually have given up and gone home if I hadn't been found before I reached the end of my tolerance.

It was on the afternoon of the second day that I'd spent in the hedgerows along the River Severn when I first saw the search party of policemen and local people. They were calling my name as they poked and prodded with sticks in all the ditches and hedges. One man came within inches of where I was hiding and even though I was deep in the thicket, I was certain he was going to see me. I held my breath and watched through half-closed eyes as he got closer and closer. Then, just as he drew level with me, someone spoke to him and although his stick touched the hedgerow directly in front of where I was crouched, he turned his head away as it did so, and when he turned back again he'd moved on past me.

Just a minute or two later, someone stopped directly in front of me again and called 'Peter!' and I knew before he turned round that it was David. You aren't really aware of discomfort, or even pain, when you're frightened, but suddenly I felt colder, wetter and hungrier than I'd ever done in my life.

'David,' I hissed, and when he didn't hear me, I said his name again, a bit louder, and made him jump.

It was all over within minutes. I was taken home by a policeman to face the music, although, in fact, my father and Flossie were surprisingly restrained in their admonishments and even went so far as to say they'd been worried about me and were glad to have me home. Then the policeman left and my father gave me a thrashing and shouted at me because of the trouble I'd caused. Flossie shouted too, while she was scrubbing my body from head to toe so roughly she tore the skin off the blisters around my waist and they formed a belt of raw, red patches.

By running away, I'd been brought to the attention of the authorities, and not long after that incident, we were visited by someone from social services.

When the man arrived at our house, one of my sisters was sent to fetch me. I opened the door of the living room tentatively, as I always did, and when Flossie spoke to me, I thought at first she was playing a spiteful joke.

'Ah, Peter!' she said, in the sort of voice you might use to greet a friend you haven't seen for a while. 'Come in, dear, and sit down.' I was edging nervously towards my stool when she laughed and waved her hand towards a chair, saying, 'Sit here, Peter.'

I glanced at the man, who must have thought I was simple, at best, the way my eyes kept darting from Flossie, to my father, to him and back again as I crept sideways, like a cautious crab, across the room. In fact, I was totally perplexed: I was never allowed to sit in any of the chairs in the living room; Flossie never called me by my name, only ever referring to me as 'the imbecile' or using some similarly contemptuous epithet; and she never, ever, called me, or anyone else, 'dear'. Although she sounded friendly – creepily so, to anyone who knew her – her eyes when she looked at me were cold and held a threat I understood.

I sat in the chair she indicated, but I kept one foot flat on the ground, just in case I had to jump up and run. My father stood near the door, behind Flossie's chair, and the stranger sat on the sofa, his briefcase open beside him. The man was a wearing a dark-brown suit and a khaki-coloured tie, and was holding some papers in one hand and a pen in the other. I think he told me his name and then he asked me a lot of questions. Did I like living in the cottage? What sort of things did I like to eat? Did I ever go to bed hungry? Did I get on well with my brothers and sisters? Was I happy? How did my parents punish me when I did something wrong? Did I behave myself at school? Did I like school? Did I have friends?

Flossie and my father were looking at me with almost identical fixed smiles on their faces and, despite what they always told me, I wasn't stupid. In fact, the performance I gave that day was worthy of an Oscar.

The man made notes of my answers – about the state of blissful happiness in which I lived with my loving family in our wonderful home – then he stood up, shook hands with my father and left. As soon as the front door had closed behind him, Flossie's friendly smile changed to smug self-satisfaction and she reached out her hand, smacked the side of my head and told me to get back to doing whatever chore I'd been doing before the man arrived.

I never saw him again, nor did I ever again sit on a chair in the living room at the cottage.

Social services might have been happy with the state of affairs in my home, but the man's visit did nothing to change the status quo. My father and stepmother continued to beat me for the slightest, most inadvertent infringement of their rules, and I continued to run away. Sometimes, I'd return after a day or two – driven home by hunger – and sometimes I'd be brought back by the police or by a well-meaning but misguided neighbour.

When a child persistently 'causes trouble' by running away, it seems logical to assume that you need to look for the reason outside the child himself. I was lucky in that some of our neighbours must have realized that, because sometimes one or other of them would take me into their house and give me a hot drink and something to eat. Once or twice, I was even allowed to stay overnight and I'd have a bath before sleeping between crisp white sheets in a warm, comfortable bed. Usually though, I'd run across the fields and find an unlocked shed or an outhouse to sleep in for a night or two. I'd made friends with most of the dogs in the village by that time, or perhaps the reason they didn't bark when they heard me was because I smelt pretty much like they did.

People in the village may have talked to each other about what was going on in Laburnum Cottage. If they did, maybe the children heard what their parents were saying and felt sorry for me, because I had a lot of friends among the local children. Whenever I ran away from home and any of them saw me, they'd tell me, in a conspiratorial whisper, to 'Wait there', and then they'd hurry into their houses and bring me out something to eat.

Flossie and my father were clearly glad to be rid of me and social services had decided to turn a blind eye – or, at least, I assume that was the case, because I find it hard to believe that the authorities didn't know what was going on, particularly as it seemed that everyone in the village did. Perhaps social services simply didn't know what to do with me, which might not have mattered too much if it hadn't been for the fact that I was beginning to retreat into a world of my own, a world that I was reluctant to let anyone else enter.

I wasn't rude or disrespectful to people – quite the opposite in fact. I'd had enough harsh, cruel words spoken to me not to want to repeat any of them myself, and I think I understood that if I wanted strangers to be nice to me, I had to be polite to them.

It was just that I wanted to be left alone, so I never encouraged conversations with anyone unless there was something I needed them to do for me. I must have given the impression of being an odd little boy. I was certainly wary, and I was always more comfortable watching things quietly from the sidelines than taking part.

I wasn't always roaming the countryside and sleeping rough, of course – someone would have been forced into taking some sort of action if I'd never gone to school at all. I just ran away when something especially bad happened at home or when I was punished particularly viciously or unjustly, but I'd always return after a night or two.

One day, after Flossie had beaten me with the poker and then kicked me, I suddenly felt I had to talk to someone. It was a feeling I didn't remember ever having had before, and once the idea entered my head, it quickly grew into something close to an obsession.

I'd heard somehow – it must have been from someone in the family but I can't think who – that a relative of my father's called Sonia Denby lived in a nearby village. I decided that instead of disappearing into the countryside, I was going to go and see her. I didn't know where the village was, but there was a signpost to it at the crossroads, so I didn't think it could be very far away.

I was nine years old and could be very determined when I needed to be. On this occasion, I was resolved to find my father's relative and tell her about the beatings and about how I felt when I woke up every morning and didn't want to get out of bed because I dreaded the start of another day. In fact I was so set on carrying out my plan that I was even prepared to risk what I knew would be a very severe punishment by taking Flossie's bicycle.

I was a light sleeper and was woken up several times every night by noises and nightmares. This particular morning I woke up very early, got up, pulled on some clothes and crept out of the cottage while everyone else was still asleep.

The bicycle was leaning against the scullery wall at the back of the house, where Flossie always left it – there was little risk of it being stolen in those days. I was used to having to be quiet when I was hiding out in the countryside, and I barely made a sound as I wheeled the bicycle into the lane, climbed on to it and began to pedal as fast as I could towards the crossroads and from there along the road to the village where I hoped I'd find Sonia Denby.

As with so many things in my young life, it was just as well I didn't know what lay ahead – in this case, how long the journey was going to be. If I *had* known that the village was at least five miles away, I might not have set off at all.

As it was a lady's bicycle, it didn't have a crossbar, which was fortunate because it was much too big for me and my feet didn't reach the pedals when I was sitting on the seat. To begin with, I wobbled and hit the curb a few times and once came very close to crashing into the hedgerow, but eventually I got the bicycle under control. The only time I *could* sit down was when I was going downhill; otherwise, I stood up to pedal, which meant that I was constantly bouncing up and down until the muscles in my legs felt as if they were on fire. When I came to a long, steep hill, I had to get off and push the bike up it, and that's when I began to snivel a bit and wonder if I was going to make it to my destination at all, or if I was going to have to turn round and go back home to face what would be the very discordant music.

Just as I hadn't thought about how far it was from my home to Sonia Denby's, I don't think I'd considered how I was going to find my father's relative once I arrived in the village. In retrospect, it was nothing short of a miracle that, with a population of maybe 4,000 people at that time, one of the several people of whom I asked the question, 'Do you know where Sonia Denby lives?' was able to answer, 'Yes.'

It wasn't until I'd leaned the bicycle against the wooden fence and pushed open the gate separating the front garden from the pavement that the thought suddenly struck me I might not be welcomed with open arms by a relative who probably didn't even know of my existence. By the time I'd summoned the courage to knock on the front door, I was half hoping no one would be at home. I felt sick. The palms of my hands were sweating and every time I tried to concentrate, I could hear a mocking voice inside my head saying, 'Why did you come here, imbecile?' I was on the point of turning and running back down the garden path when the front door opened.

To the woman who looked at me with a quizzical but not unfriendly expression, I must have appeared to be a grubby, oil-stained, uncared-for waif — which I suppose is what I was. Suddenly, determination elbowed its way through all the doubt and embarrassment: I hadn't cycled all that way simply to have the door shut firmly in my face. So, before the woman had a chance to say anything, I blurted out, 'I'm Peter Kilby. I've come on my own a really long way on a bicycle to see Sonia Denby because she's my relative.'

The words tumbled out of my mouth in an unpunctuated stream, and it must have been difficult for her to know where one ended and another began. But she smiled at me and said, 'If you can talk more slowly, I'll be able to understand what you're saying.'

So I told her again and when I'd explained more

coherently who I was and why I'd come, she shook my hand solemnly and said, 'I'm Sonia Denby.' Then she took a step back into the house and invited me in.

Chapter 6

I followed Sonia Denby into the kitchen of the little terraced house and sat at a scrubbed-wood table to drink the glass of milk she gave me. Then I answered her questions and told her a bit about my life and about how there wasn't anyone I could talk to, and when someone had mentioned my father had a relative who lived in a village not very far away, I'd decided to talk to them. 'That's you,' I added, in case she'd got a bit bogged down in what I'd been saying and hadn't understood that part of it.

'Yes, I realize that,' she told me, smiling in a sad sort of way and patting my hand.

After she'd asked me a few more questions, she stood up, rested her hand on my shoulder for a moment and said, 'What you need, Peter, is a nice hot bath.' She explained that it would help my aching muscles, but I think she might also have suggested it because I had dirty hands and oil-stained shins.

When I'd had the bath, I went back to the kitchen and Sonia made me something to eat while I continued to tell her my story. I'd never told anyone about the punishments, beatings and unkindness I'd lived

94

with for as long as I could remember, and it was as if the floodgates had opened, allowing all the misery that had been building up inside me like water in a dam to come pouring out.

'I'm going to write a letter to your father,' she told me when at last I began to run out of verbal steam. 'When he knows someone is aware of what's going on, it'll stop, particularly if I tell him that I'll go to the police if it doesn't.'

It did cross my mind that a letter like that might simply make things worse for me. But she seemed so certain that it would have the effect she described, I decided to take her word for it. After all, *I* was always a bit frightened by the stern policemen who sometimes took me home after I'd run away, so it seemed logical to assume that Flossie and my father might be too.

After sharing the secret I'd been keeping for so long, I felt almost elated, not least because it was clear that the woman I'd shared it with – a woman who had no real reason to care about me or have more than a passing interest in what happened to me – had believed what I'd told her.

When I was unburdening myself to Sonia, her husband had come into the kitchen and while she wrote her letter, he took me into the living room, where he opened a drawer in an old oak sideboard and took out a rectangular wooden box. I leaned forward as he opened the box, eager to see what was inside, and he laughed out loud at my gasp of astonishment when I saw the pistol. I'd never seen a real gun before and I was very impressed.

'Would you like to hold it?' Mr Denby asked, lifting the pistol out of the box as he spoke.

I looked at him closely, trying to decide if he was joking. But, despite his broad smile, it seemed to be a serious offer, and I nodded my head vigorously.

The pistol was so heavy I had to hold it with both my hands and, as I stood there looking at it, I felt a sudden rush of pride at the thought that I must seem like the sort of boy who could be trusted to hold a pistol.

When Sonia Denby had finished writing her letter, she folded it up and handed it to me, saying, 'You'd better go now. You need to get home before it's dark. You *will* be all right, won't you? Do you know the way?'

What I was bursting to say was that I didn't want to go home at all, ever. I wanted to stay in that nice warm house with those two kind people and never see Flossie or my father or any of my family again. But I didn't want to seem like a cry-baby. So I said that I *did* know the way, thank you. Then I took the letter, put it in the pocket of my shorts and, with a full stomach and at least some hope in my heart, I set off on the bicycle in the direction of my home.

By the time I'd turned off the main road on to the road that would take me all the way back to the village, it was almost dusk. And then it began to rain. I was anxious about arriving at the cottage late in the evening, although, in view of the trouble I'd already be in for lots of other reasons – including taking Flossie's bicycle so that she would have had to walk to the shops that morning – I don't know why I thought it would matter what time I got home. But when the rain became a torrential downpour, I was forced to stop and take shelter.

Jumping off the bicycle, I pushed it into a small wooded area at the side of the road, where I leaned it against a tree and squeezed myself under a thick hedge, managing to manoeuvre into a position that was quite comfortable, despite a few damp patches. As I sat there, waiting for the rain to ease off, the dusk slowly turned to darkness and I began to feel drowsy.

When I woke up, the rain had stopped and there was a glow in the sky that it took me a moment to realize was the rising sun. Although I was cold, I was relatively dry, apart from my right hip, which must have been directly underneath a persistent drip. I eased my hand into the sodden pocket of my shorts – and that's when I remembered the letter. I burst into tears when I saw it, all crumpled up and with blotches of blue ink where some of the words had been. After all that effort, all the hours of cycling and summoning up the courage to tell someone things I'd never dared tell anyone before, the rain had washed away some of the words that might have changed everything for me.

If I'd had anywhere else to go, I would have gone there that morning rather than going home. There wasn't anywhere else for me though, so I folded up the letter and put it into my dry, left-hand pocket. Then I wiped the tears from my dirty face on to the back of my even dirtier hand, pushed the bicycle out of the woods and on to the road, and started pedalling towards Laburnum Cottage.

I arrived home just as everyone was getting up. Whenever I was really scared, my stomach would churn and my head would feel heavy, as if it was full of something that was stopping me thinking clearly. That's how I felt that morning as I leaned the bicycle against the scullery wall and then stood in a corner of the garden at the back of the house where I knew I couldn't be seen by anyone looking out of a window.

When one of my sisters opened the back door and saw me standing there, she was as startled as I was. I quickly put my finger to my lips and whispered to her, 'Don't tell.' She just looked at me for a second with an odd expression on her face and then went back into the house, closing the door behind her and shutting me out.

It didn't really make much difference how my entry into the house was effected. I was going to have to face the music eventually. It was just that it would have been nice to have felt that my own sister was on my side – if only to the extent of not actually relishing the prospect of telling Flossie and my father that I'd come home. Suddenly, I felt completely alone.

Within seconds of my sister shutting the back door, it opened again, and this time it was my father who came out of the house, like a stampeding bull. He was bare-chested and wearing only his pyjama bottoms and he looked as if he'd been interrupted while in the process of shaving.

I'd taken Sonia's letter out of my pocket – the letter I fervently prayed was going to be my salvation – and I was clutching it tightly in my hand when my father reached out and grabbed hold of my collar.

'You . . . You've got to read this letter,' I stuttered, thrusting the damp bit of paper at him.

Without releasing his grip on my neck, my father snatched the letter out of my hand, and then he dragged me into the scullery, shouting at me and demanding to know where the bloody hell I'd been.

'I . . . I . . . I've been to see Sonia,' I told him, furious with myself for stammering and sounding frightened instead of like someone who was about to reveal an invincible weapon.

'Who the hell's Sonia?' my father shouted into my face.

'Sonia Denby, your relative.' I was desperate to get the words out before he thrashed me. 'She's going to tell the police about you if you hurt me again.'

My father snorted and gave me a shove that sent me crashing against the shelves on the wall behind me.

'What do you know about Sonia Denby?' he demanded. 'Have you been sneaking around eavesdropping on conversations that don't concern you? What did you tell her? The answer better be "nothing" or you're going to wish you hadn't poked your nose in where it doesn't belong.'

'It's in the letter,' I said, trying to convey a confidence I didn't feel. What if all that remained on the crumpled piece of paper was a series of illegible smudges of ink?

When my father raised his hand, I flinched and turned my head to the side to try to avoid taking the blow I thought was coming full in the face. But instead of punching me, he told me to, 'Stay there!' Then he walked out of the scullery and closed the door, taking the precious letter with him.

I could hear the murmur of voices in the kitchen; then Flossie shouted something and my father shouted back at her. Their heated argument continued for some time and I could tell it was a particularly serious one. Maybe enough of Sonia's letter had remained legible for them to be able to read and understand it. Part of me hoped that was the case; part of me was suddenly afraid of what Flossie and my father might do if they thought they were being threatened by someone who couldn't or wouldn't see that threat through to its conclusion.

By the time the scullery door opened again, I was shaking, both because I was cold and very tired and because I was suddenly exhausted from the constant, unremitting effort of always being afraid and never knowing what was going to happen next.

'Get yourself washed and get to bed. There'll be no school for you today.' My father's voice was harsh and his eyes were full of anger and hatred.

Although I knew I wasn't out of the woods yet – nowhere near it – I felt a rush of relief at the thought that if something bad was going to happen, and experience made it hard for me to believe that it wasn't, at least I had a reprieve for the time being. As soon as he'd finished shaving, my father would get dressed and go to work. And although that still left Flossie to contend with, with a bit of luck she'd be too busy to bother about me for at least the next couple of hours.

After washing myself quickly and not very thoroughly in cold water from the brass tap in the scullery, I ran up the stairs to my bed on the landing and was asleep before the front door closed behind the last of my siblings as they left for school. Despite being very hungry, and despite having slept in the woods during the previous night, I fell into a deep, exhausted sleep that lasted for the rest of the day.

When my father got home from work, one of my sisters was sent to tell me to get dressed and come down for my tea. I ate it, as I always did, sitting on the stool facing the wall, but by that time I was so hungry I think I'd have eaten standing on my hands in the village pond if that's what I'd been told to do.

To my surprise – and enormous relief – no one spoke to me while we were eating our tea. In fact, no one said anything much at all to anyone. Afterwards I was sent back to bed – which, to me, seemed like a blessing rather than the punishment it was supposed to be – and the next morning I got up and went to school.

Sleeping on the mattress-less, iron-framed bed on the landing, I had nowhere to put my clothes when I took them off at night except on the floor underneath it. So they were still damp and very creased when I put them on in the morning. No one at school ever mentioned my scruffy appearance, even when I sometimes turned up in the clothes I'd been wearing during a night or two spent sleeping in a hedgerow. In fact, the other children were surprisingly uncritical, the teachers were kind and did nothing to make me feel more like an outsider than I already felt, and the lady who served the school dinners always gave me an extra large helping and a wink.

Every time I returned after missing school for a day or two, my class teacher would ask me where I'd been and if I was all right. I was too afraid to tell her the truth – even after I'd summoned up the courage to talk to Sonia Denby – and although she always made sure she gave me the chance to talk about it if I wanted to, she didn't push me.

As I say, I hadn't really believed the letter would make a difference – at least, not in any good way – but for the next few weeks Flossie and my father didn't beat or punish me at all. What they did do was send me to Coventry, which meant that no one in my family spoke to me or acknowledged my existence in any way, not even by looking at me. For me, it wasn't a punishment but a relief, although I knew it couldn't last.

I wasn't directly involved in the incident that brought to an abrupt end the comparative state of peace that had reigned for a while in Laburnum Cottage. The first warning I had that anything had happened at all was when I heard Flossie and my father start to argue. Their voices quickly got louder until they were screaming abuse at each other. Then, suddenly, all hell broke loose and my father started running around the house bellowing at the top of his voice.

I'd been sitting on my bed when it all kicked off, and when I peered cautiously down the stairs, I could see that he was holding a small hatchet in his hands, which he was using to reduce to splinters anything and everything in his path. To add to the frightening confusion, Flossie was shrieking and running along behind him, darting forward every few seconds to make what appeared to be very ill-advised attempts to stop him destroying all the furniture. For Flossie and my father, fighting was an integral part of living together. At least four or five times a week, they'd shout and scream and hurl things at each other. Although my stomach always tied itself into tight little knots of anxiety when it happened, it was what I was used to. This time, however, I knew immediately that something different was going on. I waited until my father had charged like a maniacal agent of destruction into the living room and then I ran down the stairs and out of the house, followed closely by my siblings and half-sister – my stepbrothers had already moved out to live in places that were less like active war zones.

The scullery had a tiled roof, a brick chimney in the centre of its outside wall, and a drainpipe that ran from the gutter to the ground. I often used to climb up that drainpipe when danger threatened and crouch behind the chimney. It was a good hiding place, particularly when there was a fire burning in the grate and the chimney was warm. And it was where I went on that occasion, when fear sent me shinning up the drainpipe at record-breaking speed.

To any casual observer, it must have looked like a scene from a farce straight out of the Ealing Film Studios. My father ran out of the back door, around the garden and into the house again through the front door shouting, 'I'll kill the bastard. Where is he? When I find him I'm going to break every bone in his effing body. I'll kill him.' Flossie was still in hot pursuit, apparently trying to calm him down, although shouting at him in the way she was doing might not have been the best method to employ in order to achieve that end.

I was shaking and shivering behind the chimney with the blood pounding in my head when it dawned on me that *I* was the 'bastard' my father wanted to kill. I had absolutely no idea why and the realization transformed my fear into terror. I knew that if he caught me while he was so angry, he really could do me serious physical harm. And I knew, too, that Flossie wouldn't try to protect my life with anything like the same fervour with which she was attempting to protect the furniture. My only chance was to remain hidden for as long as I possibly could; certainly until my father had calmed down enough to have relinquished the hatchet.

The next time my father's circuit around the house and garden took him and Flossie past the scullery en route to the front door, my brother suddenly appeared just below where I was hiding and called my name, very quietly and urgently. As I whispered an answer, I moved my head just enough to be able to see with one eye around the side of the chimney.

'Quick! Get down here,' he hissed at me. 'Come on. We've only got a few seconds.'

I had no alternative plan, so I did as he told me and climbed quickly down the drainpipe. As soon as my feet touched the ground, he grabbed hold of my hand, dragged me towards the vegetable patch at the end of the garden, pushed me face down on to the sour-smelling earth between two rows of cabbages and sprouts, and then threw himself down beside me.

Although I was more frightened than I'd ever been in all the frightening years of my life, it was somehow comforting to know that my brother was lying next to me and that he'd taken the risk of coming to find me. It was only the second time he'd ever done anything to try to help me, and he never did anything similar again. At that moment, I was just grateful not to be alone.

We lay there, side my side and hardly daring to

breathe, for what seemed like hours, although in reality it must only have been a few minutes. Flossie and my father didn't come out of the house again, and eventually my brother whispered, 'They're upstairs, in the bedroom.' Then he lifted his hand from the back of my neck and we stood up.

'Go and wash your face,' he hissed at me as we tiptoed into the house. So I went to the scullery, scooped cold water from the tap into my hands and watched as the dirt swirled around the plughole and disappeared from sight.

While I was washing my face, I could hear the girls sneaking back into the house. I'd just picked up the towel when one of my sisters stopped in the open doorway and said angrily, 'It's all your bloody fault.' I knew she was probably right, if only because I'd learned from experience that, one way or another, everything was always my fault, although I rarely knew why. The only reason I could think of this time for my father's frenzied rage was that it might have something to do with Sonia's letter.

When I came out of the scullery, my brother was waiting for me.

'I think this is one occasion when it would be a good idea if you were to go away for a while,' he told me. 'It isn't safe for you here.'

'But why?' I asked him. 'What's happened? I haven't done anything.'

'You just need to go,' he said.

My siblings rarely looked me in the eye, but my brother held my gaze for a moment before shrugging his shoulders and repeating, 'Just go.' So, after stopping in the kitchen to snatch up a chunk of cheese and some matches, I slipped out through the back door and disappeared into the darkness.

I'd already decided before I left the house where I was going to go. There was a farm about a quarter of a mile away across the fields behind the cottage, where the farmer kept cattle and goats and where there was a metal barn that I knew contained straw, and possibly even mangels or cow-cake. I was very hungry. It was a cold night and I'd picked up the box of matches from the kitchen with the vague idea of being able to light a fire if I had to sleep out in the open; but a barn would be a much better place to spend the night than a hedgerow.

I stood just inside the barn waiting for my eyes to grow accustomed to the darkness and then I looked around me. There were straw bales in one corner and some farm implements on the ground near a long wooden bench. I knelt down in front of the bench and began to rummage through the bits and pieces on its seat, which included balls of twine, a rusty pocket knife that wouldn't open, a chipped cup and other things that had probably been useful to someone at some time. And then, amongst all the jumble, I saw a small paraffin lamp, like the one that hung in the shed behind the cottage.

I picked it up and removed the glass cover before rotating the little metal wheel at the side to turn up the wick. There was a strong smell of paraffin, which suggested that it might still contain some fuel. Putting the cover down carefully on the bench beside me, I carried the lamp over to the opposite corner of the barn, where I sat down with my back against a straw bale, put the lamp on the ground between my legs and felt in my pocket for the box of matches.

Although there wasn't much wick left, and most of what did remain was charred and brittle, it caught as soon as I touched it with a struck match. The light cast by the lamp was so bright that I quickly turned down the wick and cupped my hands around the flame in case anyone saw it – although I don't know who else might be roaming the countryside at that time on a cold night. Certainly Flossie and my father wouldn't have ventured out from the warmth of Laburnum Cottage to look for me.

The only things I was really afraid of were all contained within the walls of my own home. Out here in the countryside I was safer and, at last, I could relax – a bit. As I felt in my pocket for the piece of cheese, I could feel the knots in my stomach loosening, one by one. I sighed, lay back against the straw and watched the shadows cast around the barn by the flame of the lamp.

I don't know how long I'd been asleep – probably only seconds – when I was woken up with a start by something running across my ankles. I knew instantly that the 'something' it was most likely to be was a rat. I leapt to my feet and as I did so, I knocked the paraffin lamp with my hand and almost before it had fallen on to its side, it was spewing out liquid flame.

For a moment I just stood there, rooted to the spot by horror at the realization of what I'd done. It was like watching a burning fuse, except instead of having to wait until the flame reached the end of a wire to detonate an explosive, it was spreading across the straw and setting light to everything in its path. My mind was completely blank and I had no idea what to do. Then, through the haze of panic, some instinct told me it was already too late to change the inevitable course of events and I darted out of the barn with the speed – if not the grace – of an Olympic sprinter. I imagine the rats weren't far behind me.

About fifty yards further along the road from the barn was the rectory. When I reached it, I ran into its garden, making sure I stayed in the darkest shadows, and climbed up into the branches of a tall pine tree. I didn't need to be high above the fields in a tree to see the flames from the barn that were already lighting up the sky for what seemed to be miles around. Within minutes I could hear urgent voices and the sound of running feet, and then I saw figures on the road.

It was hard to believe that the flame from one small paraffin lamp had created the raging, crackling, devastating fire that was spreading like wind through the barn and beyond. It was a dramatic sight, and it might have been an exciting one if it hadn't been for the fact that I felt sick knowing I was to blame for what was happening – and that, in all likelihood, no one would believe I hadn't started the fire deliberately.

Chapter 7

It must have been fifteen minutes or more before I heard the loudly clanging bell of the fire engine. It arrived too late to save the barn and its contents, but at least the firemen were able to prevent the fire spreading and causing more damage than it had already done.

I stayed hidden in the pine tree until the last remaining sparks had been doused by water from the firemen's hoses and the road was empty of all the onlookers who'd been standing in huddles, their faces lit eerily by the flames that seemed to be licking the stars in the sky. Then I climbed down from the tree, sat under the cover of some bushes and tried to decide what to do next.

I knew I couldn't go home, so I needed to find somewhere to sleep for the rest of the night. Now that the adrenalin had stopped pumping at the speed of an express train around my body, I'd become aware that I was shivering: my short trousers and thin jacket were damp and offered no protection against the bitterly cold night air. Then I remembered the goat pens near the farmhouse; there weren't any other options I could think of.

As I crept along the edge of the gravel driveway that led from the farmhouse to the road, I could hear the sound of water dripping from what remained of the barn's roof, which was now just blackened sheets of corrugated iron and twisted strips of metal frame. There were still lights on in some of the rooms of the farmhouse – both upstairs and downstairs – but the curtains were drawn at all the windows as I moved stealthily through the darkness.

I'd just reached the gate to the farmyard when a dog barked. I froze with my hand on the latch, trying to work out where the sound had come from. Every muscle in my body was tense and ready for flight, and I had to force myself to stand completely still as I strained to listen. But once again the only sound I could hear was the dripping of water and the occasional rustling of a pheasant in the undergrowth on the other side of the hedge.

Then the dog barked again and when my heart eventually dropped back down into my chest, I realized, to my relief, that it was in the farmhouse and not waiting for me in the darkness on the other side of the gate. It was a relief that was short lived, however, because I knew that someone might look out of a window at any moment to see what had made the dog bark – and then they'd see me. It was time to disappear. Abandoning the idea of opening the gate, I quickly climbed over it and ran through the mud towards the goat pens.

As soon as I opened the door of one of the little wooden huts, my nostrils were filled with the comforting smell of animal warmth. It was pitch black inside the pen, but I could hear the rustling of straw, and eventually, as my eyes adapted to the darkness, I could make out the shapes of several goats.

I was fortunate as a child in being able to sleep anywhere, even when I wasn't tired. It was almost like a protective mechanism enabling me to shut down and close myself off from whatever was happening around me. It served me well that night, because as soon as I lay down in an unoccupied spot in the straw, I fell asleep.

I don't know how long I'd been sleeping when I was woken up by the sound of people talking. When I opened my eyes, I could see light through the cracks in the wooden walls of the goat pen and for a moment I was disorientated and confused. Then I heard someone call my name and I knew there was a search party out looking for me. No one had bothered to look for me on the last few occasions when I'd run away and stayed out for one or two nights. This time, though, perhaps

Flossie and my father thought the fire at the barn might have had something to do with me, and maybe they'd reported me missing in order to cover themselves if my charred remains were discovered among the ashes. I bet they'd have had to think of something really sad to stop themselves smiling if that *had* happened.

When the door of the pen opened and the early-morning light seeped in, I pressed my body down into the straw and held my breath, hoping that whoever it was wouldn't notice me. I could see a man standing in the doorway. He was wearing a tweed jacket and trousers tucked into his wellington boots and he was holding a torch, the beam from which flickered around the barn until it illuminated the corner where I was lying. I closed my eyes against the bright light and the man called out, 'He's here. I've found him.' When I opened my eyes again, I saw him turn and walk out of the pen, shutting the door behind him.

My stomach churned almost constantly when I was a child; the only thing that changed when real trouble loomed was that the churning became more energetic and the butterflies panicked and flapped their wings more vigorously. As I sat in the straw on that cold early morning, I had a feeling that something *really* bad was about to happen.

When the door of the goat pen opened again a

minute or two later, the figure of a uniformed police-man was silhouetted against the light and a voice said, 'Come on out, lad.'

'I didn't do it,' I said, scrambling to my feet and picking my way carefully among the goats. 'I mean, I *did* do it, but I didn't do it on purpose. It was an accident. I lit the paraffin lamp because I was cold and it was really dark and then all the paraffin ran out on to the straw and I couldn't . . .'

'Aye, well don't worry about that now,' the police-man interrupted me. 'There'll be plenty of time for explanations later.'

I wasn't sure whether that was a good thing or a bad one.

At the door, the policeman put his hand on my shoulder as if to steer me in the direction he wanted me to go, but quickly removed it again when I stepped out into the daylight and he saw the mud and goat droppings that covered almost every inch of my body. The smell of the farmyard accom-panied me into the police car, where I sat on a road map the policeman spread across the back seat and breathed the early-morning air through his wide-open window.

Although I didn't know it at the time, the red-brick building I was taken to was a court house, and as soon as we arrived there, I was almost frog-marched to a room that had a bath in it. The woman who bundled up my filthy, foul-smelling clothes and stayed with me while I sat in the warm water and washed away all the grime of the fire and the goat pen was kind and patient. By the time I clambered out of the bathtub, smelling of soap, my anxiety level had dropped from very high to just high.

Wearing a dressing gown several sizes too big for me and with the woman's hand resting in a friendly way on my shoulder, I allowed myself to be propelled towards a kitchen, where I was given two pieces of hot toast dripping with butter and a mug of steaming tea. After I'd eaten my breakfast, I was led down a corridor to a drab room furnished with a settee, a table and four chairs, where I was left alone for what seemed like hours.

Every now and then, a woman would open the door. She didn't say anything and she didn't come into the room; she just looked at me, nodded and then closed the door again, and I'd listen to the clip-clopping sound of her heels growing fainter as she walked away down the corridor. Eventually, the door opened again and a woman and a man came into the room.

'We're police officers,' the woman told me. 'We want to ask you some questions. Shall we sit at the table?'

I sat down on the chair she pulled out for me and she and the man sat opposite me. Their questions were all about what had happened the night before and then, abruptly, the woman asked, 'Why do you run away from home, Peter? Do you think you can explain it to us? You can tell us anything, you know. You don't have to be afraid.'

Once I started to talk, I couldn't stop. I told them about my life at home and about the time I'd spent with my grandmother and Nigel and Delia; how my stepmother had come to get me on the bus and Nigel hadn't wanted to let me go; how I'd taken Flossie's bicycle and visited Sonia Denby and then she'd written a letter to my father so that I hadn't been beaten for a while; and then how my father had flown into a rage and run around the house with a hatchet saying he was going to kill me, and my brother had told me to run away.

'And that's why I was in the barn,' I said at last. 'And when the barn burned down, I slept in the goat pen — because it was warm and because goats don't hurt you.'

Apart from interrupting a few times to ask me specific questions, the police officers just listened. Sometimes they looked angry, although they didn't seem to be angry with me, and sometimes, when I stuttered and had to rub my face with the sleeve of the dressing gown so that they wouldn't think I was a cry-baby, they smiled in an encouraging sort of way.

When I'd told them everything and felt just like

one of those limp, partially stuffed figures children take around on little carts on Guy Fawkes' night, they stood up. The woman reached across the table and patted my shoulder as she said, 'Wait here, Peter,' and then they left me alone again in the room.

A few minutes later, the silent woman came back and opened the door; this time though, she came right into the room, closed the door behind her and pulled one of the wooden chairs across the floor to where I was sitting on the settee. When she was sitting down facing me, she said, 'You won't be going home today, Peter. In fact, you won't be going home again for a while. You're going to go and stay in another home.'

She named a town I hadn't heard of and although I had no idea where it was, I felt light-headed with relief. I wasn't sorry I'd told the police officers everything, as they'd asked me to do, but while I'd been sitting alone in the room, I'd been wondering, with a growing sense of dread, what would happen to me when I was taken back to Laburnum Cottage.

I wouldn't have felt so relieved if I'd known what lay ahead.

After telling me that she was going to take me to the new home later in the afternoon, the woman gave me some books to read while I waited. She checked on me at intervals as she'd done before, again mostly without saying anything, and at lunch-time she brought me a sandwich and a glass of orange squash. After lunch, my clothes were returned to me – washed and dried and no longer smelling of goats and soiled straw.

Eventually, the door opened again and this time the woman appeared wearing a grey coat and holding a pair of gloves. 'It's time to go,' she said, and I followed her eagerly along the corridor, down the stairs and out of the building to the car park, where she unlocked the passenger door of a blue Hillman Minx and told me to get in.

It was already getting dark when we set off in the car and it was a long journey, although the fact that the woman didn't really talk to me except to ask me from time to time if I was all right might have made it seem longer than it actually was.

When we turned off the main road on to an unlit lane and then turned again almost immediately through some open wrought-iron gates on to a gravel drive, my drowsiness suddenly evaporated and I sat up straight and alert in my seat. If this was the driveway to the house I was going to be living in, I was impressed.

As the car swept round a circular courtyard at the end of the driveway, its headlamps fell like spotlights on a large, imposing but rather forbidding-looking building. I had only a vague memory of the house my godmother and her husband had lived in, but I was sure that this one was even bigger. Lights were on in several of the downstairs rooms and the light shining through the stained glass in the windows on either side of the front door made it look almost like a massive church.

The butterflies in my stomach were flapping their wings frantically as if trying to escape and I suddenly had a sense of foreboding, which cast a shadow over my small excitement and sent it scurrying for cover.

'Come on, Peter. It's all right.' The woman had got out of the car and was holding open my door. I knew I didn't have any choice other than to do as I was told. I swallowed hard, climbed out of the car and stood beside her as she rang the front-door bell.

The man who opened the door greeted the woman by name and smiled at her in a friendly way. He didn't look at me or take any notice of me at all and I kept close to the woman as he led us across an open hallway, down a narrow corridor and into a large room. In the centre of the room there was a heavy wooden desk covered in papers, some of which were stacked in tall, neat piles while others were spread out across its surface in what appeared to be random disarray.

It wasn't the sort of home I'd imagined it would be: there was no sign that it was lived in by a family. In fact, it didn't appear to be a home at all; it was more like a school or an office building.

The man and woman stood talking to each other for a few minutes; then they shook hands and she smiled at me as she said, 'I'm going now, Peter. You'll be well taken care of here. Be a good boy.' As if her words made the man aware of my presence for the first time, he turned to me and said, quite pleasantly, 'Stay there.' Then he followed the woman out of the room, and that's when I finally understood that she was leaving me there. Despite the fact that she'd barely spoken to me all day, I felt very much alone.

When the man walked back through the door into the office where I was waiting, as I'd been told to do, it was apparent that his attitude had changed completely. I'd seen the same abrupt about-face in Flossie and my father enough times to recognize it for what it was. Whenever someone came unexpectedly to the door of the cottage, they were charming and effusively friendly. But as soon as the visitor had walked away and the door had been closed behind them, their smiles disappeared, as if at the flick of a switch, and they reverted to their more usual glaring, bad-tempered hostility.

I recognized the bullying tone of the man's voice, too, as he told me, 'So, you're the boy who runs away from home, are you? Well, I can assure you of one thing: you won't be running away from here.' Then he turned on his heels and walked out of the room again, calling to me over his shoulder as he did so, 'Come with me, boy.'

His footsteps echoed loudly on the tiled floor as I followed him along the corridor and then up a narrow staircase to a dimly lit landing. All the doors off the landing were closed and I could sense a strange, oppressive atmosphere in the house, almost as if, behind every door, people were listening.

Because of the silence, I assumed that the man and I were the house's only inhabitants – until he opened one of the doors and I could see, in the light from the landing, that the large room was full of beds, and in almost every bed there was a child.

'That's yours,' the man told me, pointing to the bed nearest the door on the right. He spoke loudly, clearly not concerned in case the sound of his voice woke up the sleeping children.

Folded up on the bed he'd indicated was a pair of blue-and-white striped pyjamas. 'Put them on,' he barked at me, 'and then give me your clothes. Hurry up, boy. I've got better things to do than stand here waiting for you all night.'

He watched impassively as I got undressed and when I handed him my pathetic little bundle of clothes, he said, 'Now get into bed and go to sleep. I'll talk to you in the morning.' Before I had time to climb in between the icy sheets, he'd walked out of the room and shut the door, and I stood in the darkness listening to the diminishing sound of his footsteps on the stairs.

When the house was quiet again, I thought about everything that had happened in the last twenty-four hours and about what might be going to happen tomorrow and on all the tomorrows that would come after it. The not-quite-closed curtains at the window allowed just enough moonlight into the room for me to be able to see the other beds and the outlines of the sleeping children – or, at least, the children I thought were sleeping, because one by one, the boys in the beds nearest to mine sat up.

'What's your name?' one of them asked and, before long, questions were flying at me from every corner of the room.

When someone hissed urgently, 'Shush,' the room fell instantly silent as everyone strained to listen. After a few seconds, the boy in the bed next to mine spoke again. 'That's Bongo,' he said, 'the bloke that brought you in. Bongo the Finger. Well, Mr Cowley to his face.'

'Why Bongo the Finger?' I asked.

'Bongo because of the noise he makes as he stomps around the place,' another boy cut in. 'He does it on purpose, so you think you'll always hear him coming. Then at night he creeps around without his shoes on, trying to catch us out.' He gave a derisive snort. 'He's a nasty piece of work, no mistake. But he's not as clever as he thinks he is. Or maybe we're not as stupid as he thinks *we* are.'

'And finger?' I asked.

A couple of the boys sniggered, and then the boy in the bed next to mine said, 'You'll find out, if you stay here long enough.'

I was grateful for the friendly way they were talking to me, and my last thought before I fell into an exhausted sleep was that this new 'home' might not be so bad after all.

It seemed that only a few minutes had passed when I was startled out of a deep sleep by a woman's voice calling, 'Everybody up.' Still only half awake, I pushed back the blankets and swung my legs over the side of the bed. The woman who opened the door and followed her voice into the room was short and stocky – similar in build, in fact, to Flossie, although not as heavy-looking as my stepmother. The other boys were already shuffling into line in the middle of the room and when I stood up to join them, the woman pointed an almost square finger at me and said, 'Not you! You stay there.'

I sat down again on the bed and watched the other boys, shivering in their pyjamas, file silently out of the room past the woman, who stood in the open doorway saying, 'I'll be checking. So you better make sure your ablutions are thorough.' Although I had no idea what ablutions were, the tone of her voice left me in no doubt that it was no idle threat.

When the last boy had shuffled out of the room, the woman turned back to me and said, 'I'm Miss Farley. You can call me by my name or you can call me Miss.'

'Yes, Miss,' I answered politely, trying to sound like the sort of boy who wouldn't cause anyone any trouble.

'Good. Well then, come with me.'

She led the way into a bathroom where soon every icy-cold surface was covered in condensation as hot water ran into the bathtub. Two baths in two days! Surely there hadn't been enough time for any new dirt to accumulate since the last one, although I wasn't going to argue. I took off my pyjamas, dropped them on the floor at the side of the room, put one hand on the edge of the cold iron bathtub and lowered myself slowly into the water.

While I rubbed carbolic soap on to the rough flannel Miss Farley had given me and washed every inch of my body – paying particular attention to the back of my neck, as instructed – she sat on a little wooden chair, watching me through narrowed eyes. When I was as clean as I was going to get, I stepped out of the bath and she handed me a towel and, after I'd dried myself, doused me liberally with a white powder that made me sneeze. Then, leaving me standing there shivering like some goose-pimpled ghost, she walked out of the bathroom and returned a few seconds later with a pile of clothes.

'Put these on,' Miss Farley told me, handing me a set of underwear, a pair of socks, a dark-blue shirt, a grey jumper and a pair of slightly darker grey shorts. She left the room again while I was getting dressed and this time returned holding a pair of boots and some shoes.

'These are for every day,' she said, thrusting the boots into my hands. 'And these are for Sundays only.' She dropped the shoes into the crook of my outstretched arms. 'Hurry up now. You're keeping everyone else waiting.'

Dressed in my new clothes, I followed Miss Farley into the corridor, where at least twenty children were already standing in line. As soon as I'd joined the end of the line, it started to move down the stairs and into a large room with a wooden floor – which I found out later was called the common room – where Miss Farley began her morning check.

Copying what the other boys did, I held out my hands palms upwards as she walked slowly along the line, turning them over when she paused in front of me. When she started again from the beginning, it soon became clear that her main obsession was what she called, with obvious distaste, 'tide marks' on necks. Standing in front of each boy, she put her sturdy hand on the top of his head and pressed down, forcing him to bend his neck so that she could examine the back of it and behind his ears. When she'd finished, she returned to the beginning of the line once more, and as she walked along it this time, she grasped each boy's chin between her thumb and index finger, jerked it upwards abruptly and turned his head from side to side as she continued her single-handed but determined battle against 'tide marks'.

Woe betide any boy who was foolish enough to think he could get away with doing a less than perfect job. Even the faintest, most shadowy hint of dirt would be detected by Miss Farley's eagle eye and, as she thumped the reprehensible reprobate on the back of the neck, she'd bark, 'Again!' and he'd scuttle out of the room to wash the offending part.

It wasn't just our hands, faces, necks and ears that had to be spotlessly clean, however: our boots had to be polished, our shirts tucked into our shorts and our socks pulled up. At least I didn't have to worry about the shine on my new boots on that first morning.

By the time Miss Farley had finished her meticulous inspection, the hands on the clock above the mantelpiece in the common room were at seven o'clock. My stomach was rumbling and I was looking forward to breakfast. But first there were chores to be done.

I was put to work with two other boys in the kitchen, helping the cook – although in reality I think we were more of a hindrance than a help. Some of the other boys had household tasks to do and some were sent out into the grounds to feed the chickens. The food, when it finally came that first morning, was plentiful and good, as were all of the three meals we were given every day.

It didn't take me long to learn what was expected of me, and I soon settled in and got used to the rules and routine. As well as a residential children's home, Pelham was a school and every weekday after breakfast, we attended lessons in the house – and I learned just how far behind I was in my education.

On Saturdays, we got up at the usual time and did our tasks, but were then free for the rest of the day to play – outside in the extensive grounds of the house when the weather was good, or inside when it was raining, in one of three rooms that had been allocated for reading, playing board games and making models from kits. On Sundays, we went to church after breakfast, to Sunday school in the afternoon and to church again in the evening. Whatever the weather, we walked in pairs in a crocodile – wearing our polished Sunday shoes – to the church in the village and back again after each service.

Some of the boys muttered and protested about being forced to attend church, but I didn't mind.

Except for the brief periods I'd spent in Wales and Cheltenham, everything in my life had been chaotic and unpredictable, and it was good to have some regularity in it at last. I liked knowing exactly what was expected of me and what was going to happen at any given moment.

In addition to Miss Farley and the cook, the staff at the home included some helpers who worked in the kitchen and a gardener, who moved around the grounds at a snail's pace, appeared to be extremely old and treated all the boys with the same high degree of suspicion. All the staff members lived in the village, except for Bongo, his wife and their twelve-year-old daughter, who lived in a flat in the main house.

On the third morning I was there, I was summoned to Bongo's office, where he asked me how I was getting on. 'Fine, sir,' I told him, although actually I was a good deal better than fine. I was clean; I had boots and shoes that fitted me; I'd been given a haircut that, by removing my thick, unruly curls, had made me look like a normal boy instead of a very small but otherwise archetypal crazy professor; I was having good, regular meals; and I was sleeping in a clean, comfortable bed with a mattress and sheets. In fact, I was actively enjoying my new life.

'Well, just make sure you behave yourself and don't do anything that's going to land you in hot water,' Bongo told me, in a begrudging tone of voice, as if he didn't really think I deserved to be 'fine'. And then the interview was over.

It's funny how some apparently inconsequential things stick in your mind, whereas you forget some of the other, more significant, ones. I think perhaps I've remembered the incident with the little injured mouse because I felt guilty about it afterwards and maybe also because, later, I could see some parallels with my own behaviour.

The mouse had been raked up with some leaves in the garden at Pelham and it was so weak it didn't resist at all when I picked it up, carried it into the house and put it in a small cardboard box. After I'd made a few holes in the lid of the box so that the mouse could breathe, I went back out into the garden to gather some leaves and grass. When I dropped what I'd collected into the box to make a soft bed, the poor little thing didn't move and for a moment I thought it might have died.

It was a Sunday and we always had a slice of cake with our tea on Sundays. When no one was looking, I broke off a piece of mine and slipped it into the pocket of my trousers. I couldn't wait for the meal to be over, and when at last we were told that we could leave the table, I hurried back to the dormitory.

Lifting the box carefully out of its hiding place, I sat on my bed and opened the lid just enough to be able to put the bit of cake inside, crumbling it between my fingers as I did so. And that's when the mouse bit me. When it sank its tiny, razor-sharp teeth into my finger, I rammed the lid down on to the box and looked in angry disbelief at the blood oozing out of the wound. Then I picked up the box, ran out into the garden and hurled it across the lawn.

As it hit the ground, the lid flew off and the apparently fully recovered mouse scuttled away into a pile of leaves, leaving me nursing my bleeding finger and my resentment for its ingratitude. I'd tried to help it and in return it had bitten me.

I was sorry later that I'd thrown the box across the grass: I knew what it was like to be frightened and not to know who, if anyone, you can trust, so that you react instinctively to try to defend and protect yourself. And I don't suppose, when it comes to basic instincts, a frightened little mouse out of its natural environment is very different from a frightened little boy who finds himself in a similar situation.

Chapter 8

The boys at Pelham often talked about Bongo and although I hadn't seen it for myself, they said he sometimes came into the dormitory late at night, woke someone up – not always the same boy – and took him to his office. They sniggered when they told me, but when I asked, 'Why would he want to see a boy in the middle of the night?' they just shrugged and said, 'If you're here long enough, you'll find out.' And, as it turned out, I *was* there long enough.

I'd been at the home for about three months when I woke up one night with a start. Despite having settled in well to my new life and thriving on its regularity and stability, I still had nightmares. So at first I thought I was dreaming. Then I opened my eyes and realized that Bongo really was standing beside my bed, shaking my shoulder and whispering at me, 'Get up, quietly. I need to see you in my office.'

As I padded along the corridor behind him, still bemused by sleep, I remember being struck by the fact that he wasn't wearing any shoes. In his stockinged feet, he somehow seemed less forbidding than he normally did. Even so, my stomach was churning as I tried to think what I'd done wrong. I knew it must be something pretty serious to warrant being summoned in the middle of the night; I just couldn't think what it was.

In Bongo's office, the chair that was always behind the desk was now in front of it and he sat down on it. I was standing, shivering with cold and nervous anxiety, near the door he'd closed behind us, and he beckoned me towards him, smiled – in fact, it was more like a grimace than a smile – and said, 'Come over here, Peter.' It was the first time he'd ever used my name – normally he referred to all of us as 'Boy' – and for some reason it made me feel more apprehensive rather than less.

I walked warily across the large-patterned rug and stood where he indicated beside his chair. I didn't have any understanding at all of why he'd brought me there, and I was completely taken by surprise when he reached out his arm, put it around my waist, spun me round so that I was facing away from him and then pulled me down to sit on his knee. Except for my grandmother and Delia in Cheltenham, and the time when the iron weight fell off the top of the shed door on to my head and Dr Margaret bathed my cut, I had no memory of ever sitting on anyone's lap. Sitting on Bongo's felt completely different from those other times. He'd startled me and made me feel wrong-footed and uncomfortable, so that my instinct was to resist. And when he put his hand between my legs and started touching me, I leapt to my feet as if I'd been scalded and shouted, 'No!'

It was Bongo's turn to be startled. 'Get back to bed,' he told me crossly, as if it had been *my* idea to wake up in the middle of the night and go to his office. 'Go back to your bed and behave yourself or there'll be trouble.' I didn't need telling twice. I had my hand on the doorknob before the last word was out of his mouth.

I lay awake in bed for a long time that night, puzzling over what had happened and trying to understand why I felt as if I'd just had a very lucky escape. The experience – as inexplicable and brief as it had been – had so unnerved and unsettled me that I no longer felt safe at the home, and I began, once more, to think about running away.

On the right-hand side at the end of the dormitory, just past the last bed, were two glass doors that opened on to a balcony – except that they weren't ever opened and were always kept locked. Above the doors there was an oblong window with an arm-shaped catch, and it was through that window that I decided to make my exit.

I'd learned from the bitter experience of living with Flossie and my father that when I felt threatened, it was a good idea to trust my instincts and not try to convince myself that everything would be all right: it very rarely was. Instead of hoping for the best, it was sensible to assume the worst, and to get out and away before the worst happened.

I planned to leave Pelham on the first Friday after the night Bongo woke me up. I didn't say anything to anyone about what I was going to do. I just made sure I ate a good supper and then I lay awake in my bed for what seemed like hours, until I was certain all the other boys were asleep, before getting up and dressed.

As I was creeping down the middle of the room towards the window, one of the boys stirred and said something. I froze, biting my lip and waiting for him to speak again. But he must have been having a dream, and eventually I continued my tiptoed journey. There was an unused bedside locker at the end of the room, which I moved as quietly as I could into position against the glass doors. Climbing on to the locker was the most difficult part, and I almost brought it crashing to the ground on top of me, which would not only have woken up every boy in my dormitory, but probably also everyone in the entire building. In fact no one woke up, which was doubly surprising to me because it meant they couldn't hear the loud thudding noise my heart was making.

Standing on the locker, it was relatively easy to

reach the window, open it and climb out. The tricky bit was preventing it swinging shut with a bang as I lowered myself down on to the flat roof of the adjacent laundry room. As soon as my feet touched the surface, I crouched down in the darkness, listening and praying that lights wouldn't suddenly come on in all the windows around me. No one stirred, and after a few seconds I inched my way towards the edge of the roof, felt for the drainpipe and climbed carefully down it. Then I ran across the grass towards the hedge that bordered the lane.

As I scrambled through the bushes, I felt a sense of exhilaration: I'd made it! When I thought about exactly what it was I'd achieved, however, it seemed like a hollow victory. I hadn't escaped from a miserable, violent existence punctuated by vicious physical punishments; I was leaving friends, a school I enjoyed going to, and a well-ordered daily life that made me feel safe and secure – most of the time. It was too late now though: as soon as I'd opened the window, I'd committed to running away, and there was no going back.

I walked quickly along the lane, turned on to the main road and, following the route we took to church three times every Sunday, ended up in the village. There were no lights on in any of the houses, and it seemed safe to stop and sit on the wooden bench on the village green for a few moments while I got my bearings and decided – belatedly perhaps – what I was going to do next.

I don't think I fell asleep, although that's the only thing that would explain why I didn't hear the police car until it had stopped behind me and a man in a trilby hat had got out of it. It was too late to try to make a run for it – I didn't want to be in any more trouble than I was already in. So when he opened the back door of the car and said, 'Come on, Peter; in you get,' I got up from the bench and slid on to the seat behind the uniformed policeman who was at the wheel.

I hadn't seen the man in the hat before, but he seemed to know me, and when he got back into the passenger seat of the car, he turned round to face me and asked, 'Why did you run away? Everyone said you'd settled in and were doing well. So what happened?'

'It was because of Bon . . . Mr Cowley,' I told him. 'The other boys said things about him.' I didn't add, as I might have done, that they were things I hadn't understood. I just said, 'Then he woke me up and made me sit on his knee and I didn't like it.'

When I said the words out loud, it sounded like a pathetic reason for running away. But running away was what I'd always done; I didn't know any other way to deal with feeling trapped and unhappy. Any emotions I hadn't actually managed to shut down completely, I'd encased in steely determination and buried somewhere deep inside me to try to protect them from further damage. So when Bongo made me feel threatened and insecure, I'd responded in the only way I knew. A little boy who has to pretend he doesn't care isn't always going to make what other people might consider to be rational decisions. And I must have felt strongly about what had happened, because I added defiantly, 'If you send me back there, I'll run away again.'

I couldn't work out how they'd discovered so quickly that I'd left the home, until someone told me that one of the boys had woken up, seen me disappearing through the dormitory window and raised the alarm. Obviously I hadn't been as clever or as quiet as I thought I'd been.

I had my wish though, and I wasn't taken back to the home that night. Instead, I was driven to a police station, where I was put in a cell – with the door unlocked – and given a mug of tea. When I'd drunk it, I lay down on the hard, narrow shelf-like bed, pulled the blanket up to my chin and fell asleep.

I'd come full circle – it wasn't the first time I'd been taken to a police station after I'd run away – and I felt disappointed and anxious. I knew it was my fault I was there, but although what had happened when Bongo woke me up didn't seem to be such a terrible thing when described after the event, some instinct told me he wasn't to be trusted.

When I woke up the next morning, a policewoman was standing beside me holding another mug of tea and a bowl of steaming porridge. After I'd eaten, I had a wash and was taken into the main room in the police station, where I was told I wouldn't be going back to the children's home at all.

'You're going to a small town not very far away from where your family live,' the policeman said.

My heart started to thud with excitement. 'Am I going to live with Sonia?' I asked, holding my breath while I waited for the answer.

'Who's Sonia?' the policeman asked.

'Sonia Denby,' I answered, the excitement already beginning to die. 'She's my father's relative. I went to see her and she wrote him a letter.'

'No, you're not going to live with Sonia.' The policeman sounded sympathetic. 'You're going to another home. And you'd better behave yourself this time, lad. If you keep on running away, you're going to keep on getting into trouble. You understand that, don't you?'

If I'd been able to articulate the thought, I'd have told him that trouble was what I was always trying to run away *from*.

Tyndale House was another large, imposing building at the end of a driveway off a village lane deep in the countryside. It was a residential school for naughty boys – although I didn't know that until later. I suppose, to the powers that be, that's what I was – a naughty boy; but I wasn't ever 'naughty' on purpose.

Moving to Tyndale House was very much a case of jumping out of the frying pan into the raging fire. The commandants of this particular camp were a couple in their forties called Mr and Mrs Harrison. Physically, they were the complete opposites of each other: she was very thin and quite tall, while he was short and immensely fat. In terms of their characters, however, they were like two nasty, spiteful, bullying peas in a pod.

I was ten years old when I was taken to Tyndale House and I'd already accepted the fact that living in this or some other children's home was to be my life for the forcseeable future. At least it was better than living with Flossie and my father: so far, no one had beaten me with a poker or nailed my feet to the floor.

There were about thirty children in the house when I arrived, all of them boys between the ages of six and twelve. We all had problems of one sort or another and, as I don't think people in those days were interested in delving into the minds and experiences of emotionally disturbed children, the idca seemed to be simply to contain us so that we didn't irritate or inconvenience the rest of the world.

Instead of trying to solve our problems, society relied on people like the Harrisons to rule the potentially unruly with iron fists in iron gloves.

Apart from the Harrisons, there were three other members of staff at Tyndale House, all of whom lived out and didn't work at weekends. Fortunately, one of them, a woman called Mrs Lewis, was very nice. It was clear that she didn't approve of the way we were treated by the Harrisons, although I suppose she needed the job and didn't dare oppose them openly. Mrs Lewis always spoke to me kindly and listened to me sympathetically, as I imagined my real mother would have done. So at least there was one adult who seemed to like me and who I felt I could trust.

Except on the occasions when one or other of the Harrisons was venting their bad temper on us, life at the home was fairly routine. Every morning we did our allotted chores, which consisted mostly of cleaning; then, on weekdays, we had our school lessons, after which we did more chores and homework. On Saturdays we did gardening jobs in the morning and then had free time in the afternoon. And on Sundays we attended two church services and Sunday school, as we'd done at Pelham.

On Saturday afternoons, some boys would go to the common room to play board games or build elaborate machines out of Meccano. Others, usually including me, played outside on the large lawn at the back of the house or in the woods, where we'd collect fir cones and make them into bolas – I became a bit of an expert with a bola and slingshot.

Looking back on that time now, the one 'positive' thing I can say about Mr and Mrs Harrison is that they were nothing worse than bullies. I don't mean by that that bullying isn't harmful and sometimes dangerous; it can – and does – cause immense misery and damage to both children and adults, as I know only too well from my own experiences. It was just that, having spent a lifetime being bullied, it had become the devil I knew. And it was the unknown – such as whatever Bongo had had in mind when he'd woken me up that night – that made me feel most threatened and uneasy.

The regime at Tyndale House was strict, and to ensure they kept control of all the children in their care, the Harrisons used the tried and tested technique of setting one boy against another. I quickly learned that of all the many things it was best not to do there, top of the list was saying anything derogatory about the couple, even to boys I thought were my friends. You could earn brownie points from the Harrisons by snitching on another boy who'd criticized or mocked them; and when they targeted a boy, you were just relieved it wasn't you. Having escaped from being punched and kicked by Flossie and my father, I was often subjected to similar treatment by the Harrisons, and I witnessed many physical assaults on other boys too. The trouble was, I always fought back, which Mrs Harrison, particularly, considered to be a bonus. She'd almost cackle with delight when my resistance provided her with the very small amount of justification she needed to give me an even more severe and prolonged beating.

Sometimes, it seemed that a boy would be punished for no reason at all other than because it gave the Harrisons a sense of satisfaction to remind us that they were in charge. And although they were indisputably in charge of *us*, they sometimes seemed to lose control of themselves, which is what happened one weekend when we were all summoned to the common room.

As we all filed into the room, Mr Harrison told a small thin boy called Terry to step out of the line and as soon as Mrs Harrison had closed the door, he started punching and kicking him. Terry was taken completely by surprise and when he fell on the ground as if he'd been pole-axed, Mr Harrison just kept on kicking him. It was surreal, like some awful dream or like watching a horrible scene from a film: Mr Harrison was shouting and swearing and Terry was screaming, and every time he screamed, he was kicked even harder until he was, quite literally, being booted like a human football around the room.

The boys at the home weren't saints by any means; many of us were troubled and some could be quite aggressive or mouthy. But, apart from the occasional shocked gasp, none of us made a sound as we watched in open-mouthed disbelief. My own immediate thought – and I'm sure I wasn't the only boy thinking it – was that I was glad *I* wasn't the one who'd done whatever Terry had done to warrant such a brutal kicking. In fact though, I can't think of anything that anyone could do that would actually *warrant* an attack like that.

It wasn't long before my sense of relief turned to panic, because I was certain that Mr Harrison was going to kill Terry. It was a certainty that raised a difficult dilemma for me: should I keep out of it and stay safe, or should I hurl myself at Mr Harrison and try to stop him murdering the unfortunate boy? Perhaps it was a choice I wouldn't have to make, because, surely, Mrs Harrison would intervene, if only to prevent her husband being sent to prison for kicking to death one of the children in his care. I glanced across the room to where she was standing by the window with her arms folded across her chest and a spiteful smile on her face. Clearly Terry's salvation didn't lie with her.

At one end of the common room was a row of heavy wooden lockers where the board games and other odds and ends were stored. The lockers were quite deep and maybe two feet high, with short legs that created a gap of about six inches underneath them. It would have seemed impossible for anyone other than a very small child to squeeze into a space like that, but, somehow, Terry managed it. Scrabbling like a frantic, panic-stricken animal and leaving a trail of blood behind him on the floor, he squashed his body under the lockers and then pressed himself against the far wall.

Every boy in the room was holding his breath as Mr Harrison tried to reach into the space and grab hold of Terry. When he realized he wasn't going to be able to pull the boy out, he vented his fury by repeatedly kicking the locker near Terry's head. Then he turned and shouted at us, 'Let that be a warning to all of you bastards. You!' He pointed a fat finger at one of the boys and then at the blood on the floor. 'Get that mess cleaned up.'

He was breathing heavily as he spoke – like unfit people do when they've over-exerted themselves – and his face was the colour of bruised beetroot. I'd never seen him so angry before, and it was the first time I'd heard any member of staff swear. He'd made his point though: I was certainly duly warned. The problem was that I don't think any of us knew what Terry had done to have elicited Mr Harrison's uncontrolled fury. So, instead of being able to make a mental note not to do the same thing, the incident merely served to increase my already substantial sense of insecurity. No doubt it also increased the resentment all the boys felt towards the Harrisons and towards every other adult who'd ever bullied and hurt them.

There was one positive outcome, however, because witnessing Terry's kicking had created a bond among the boys, if only a temporary one. When the Harrisons left the common room, banging the door shut behind them, we all worked together to help Terry extricate himself from under the lockers and then to clean his blood off the floor.

Now that the acute panic which had enabled him to squeeze into such a small space had subsided, Terry had quite a struggle getting out again. When he eventually did, I was shocked by the way he looked. His face was swollen and covered in blood and red patches, which were already starting to turn a dark blue-black colour, and his clothes were torn where he'd caught them on the rough underside of the lockers.

Fortunately, what happened to Terry was a relatively rare occurrence. We all accepted that we'd be kicked and punched by the Harrisons on a fairly regular basis, but they didn't often take it to such extremes. I never did find out what Terry had done that day; I doubt whether he knew himself. Whatever it was, it wasn't anything that deserved such a dangerously vicious punishment.

I was a quick learner, and it didn't take me long after arriving at Tyndale House to realize that it was best to keep my mouth shut and do as I was told. In fact, doing what I was told to do was relatively easy; it was keeping my mouth shut that was sometimes the difficult part.

The Harrisons saw me in the same light they saw all the boys in their tender care: as a trouble-maker who refused to conform and an emotional/behavioural misfit on whom it wasn't worth wasting either time or effort. At the age of ten, having experienced kindness on what amounted to just a matter of days since my mother had died when I was two, I accepted their view of me. Everyone had apparently given up on me, and I think I gave up on myself too. If you pretend for long enough that you're tough and don't care about anyone or anything, you start to become the person you're pretending to be, superficially at least.

I ran away from Tyndale House twice, but I only went as far as the wooded part of the garden, where I slept for the rest of the night before returning the next morning to face my punishment. Then, one cold, wet day, after I'd been there for about eight months, I was summoned to the office and Mr Harrison told me I'd be leaving the home later that afternoon.

'Where am I going?' I asked him. 'And why? Why am I leaving?' It wasn't that I'd be sorry to go, but as I hadn't run away or done anything that had landed me in any sort of trouble for ages, I couldn't understand what the reason might be for moving me on so abruptly.

'All you need to know is that you're leaving,' snapped Mr Harrison. 'Now go and pack your bag.' His voice conveyed all the sympathy and understanding he felt – which was, as it always was, precisely none. No one else could tell me anything either, or wouldn't. So I shrugged my shoulders and said I was glad to be leaving and I didn't care where I was going because anywhere would be better than there. But the truth was that I was scared.

Chapter 9

When I'd packed my bag – which didn't take long, as I had very few items of clothing or other possessions – I snuck into the kitchen to say goodbye to Mrs Lewis. For a boy who didn't care about anything, I was surprisingly tearful when she pressed my head against her ample bosom and told me she was going to miss me. I told her I'd miss her too, but before I walked out of the kitchen, I squared my shoulders, lifted my chin and hoped that the expression on my face conveyed the proper degree of bored indifference.

After lunch, a young woman came to collect me, and when I'd said goodbye to some of the boys who'd become my friends, I climbed into the passenger seat of her car and left Tyndale House behind me for ever.

At the end of the driveway, the woman turned left, in the direction of the village where my father's relative lived, according to the signpost, and I asked her excitedly – as I'd asked the policeman a few months earlier, 'Am I going to live with Sonia?'

'So you *can* speak!' The woman laughed. 'I was beginning to wonder. And in answer to your question: you'll have to wait and see.' She smiled at me and I could feel some of the tension that had clenched my hands into tight little fists seeping out of me.

All these years later I can still remember that young woman's face in every detail, particularly her smile. In fact I can remember the faces of all the women who were ever kind to me when I was a child. I didn't see a photograph of my mother until I was an adult, so I think I imprinted their faces on my mind in the empty space where my own mother's should have been.

We can't have been in the car for more than about half an hour when we turned off the main road, drove through two stone pillars and stopped on a gravelled courtyard in front of a large Victorian house. The house looked vaguely familiar, like the indistinct memory of something I'd seen in a dream, and so did a small cottage on the other side of the courtyard. But the only thing I knew for certain about it was that it wasn't where Sonia Denby lived, as I'd hoped it would be.

I waited in the car until the woman came round to open the passenger door and said cheerfully, 'Come on, Peter. We're here.' When I got out, she caught hold of my hand and squeezed it as if to reassure and encourage me, and I managed a wan smile as I walked beside her across the courtyard.

We were still a few feet away from the cottage when the front door opened and a woman came out to greet us. Sometimes, when you see something totally unexpected, your mind can't make sense of it immediately, which was what happened that day, when my grandmother came hurrying towards us with a huge grin on her face. The large, not-quite-familiar Victorian house was where my godmother, Dr Margaret, and her husband lived. It turned out that when Dr Margaret had heard I was in a children's home not very far away, she'd offered my grandmother a cottage on the estate so that I could go and live with her and she could look after me.

I know my grandparents had been quite well off before my grandfather died, so I don't know what had happened to leave my grandmother without money. She'd had to rent out rooms to Delia and Nigel in her flat in Cheltenham in order to make ends meet, and in lieu of rent on the cottage she'd agreed to work as a cleaner at the big house a few days a week.

It was Dr Margaret who'd made all the arrangements that had enabled me to leave Tyndale House. I was already grateful to her because of how kind she'd been to me after my mother died and Flossie moved into the bungalow, and I'll be grateful until my dying day for what she did for me and my grandmother. Although I was returning to the village my mother had taken me home to when I was just a few days old, I was being given a fresh start and a chance to live with someone who loved me. It was more than I could ever have hoped for.

For the next few months, I lived in the cottage with my grandmother and went to school in a nearby town. Of course, I wasn't instantly transformed from troubled child to 'a good boy' like the one in Robert Louis Stevenson's poem (see page 255). I was stubborn, didn't respond well to orders, found it difficult to trust people, and everything I said was liberally seasoned with slang words. I didn't actually do anything really naughty, however, and I didn't ever run away. It was just that I had a chip on my shoulder, which had developed over several years and sometimes made me behave like a fool. I'm sure there were times when my poor grandmother despaired of ever being able to do anything more than whittle away its edges.

In reality, those months I spent with my grandmother changed everything, even though that might not have been apparent to anyone at the time. I'd been heading along a road that would probably have led me into a life on the periphery of society. But because of what my grandmother did for me – with the help of the Colonel and Dr Margaret – I began to see that there was a better road to take, a road I believe my mother would have chosen for me if she'd lived.

Dr Margaret and the Colonel always stopped to talk to me whenever they saw me. The Colonel would boom at me in a jovial way and say, 'Well now, young man, and how are you?' And he'd listen when I told him. He had a big white moustache, a ramrod-straight back and a voice that would have carried to every corner of the largest parade ground. It was the stories he used to tell me – about his life in the army and about the time he spent in the Royal Lancers in India – that made me realize there was a whole world beyond my own very small experience, and it was those stories that gave me the urge to travel.

Looking back on it now, I think that was their intention: to make me understand that the world was an exciting place and there were other ways of living which were as different as it was possible for them to be from the way Flossie and my father had chosen to live their lives. My grandmother, Dr Margaret and the Colonel taught me many other things too, and by the time I started at the local secondary modern school, I felt confident in a way I'd never felt before, which enabled me to settle in and make friends. There was still a chip on my shoulder – it had been eight years in the making, so it wasn't going to disappear overnight – but it now really was a chip rather than a rock the size of Gibraltar, as it had been.

My previously very narrow horizons were expanded even further at the school, where I learned about Wordsworth and Keats and read the marvellous poem 'The Brook' by Alfred Lord Tennyson (see page 256), which gave me a love of poetry that has stayed with me ever since. At home, my grandmother encouraged me to listen to classical music on her wireless and let me play her piano, which almost filled the little sitting room at the cottage. I didn't play properly, of course; I just tinkered around trying to pick out the notes of tunes I'd heard.

One of the most significant aspects of the way my grandmother treated me was that she never shouted at me. I must often have done things that were, at best, frustrating for her – after all, I'd only ever lived in a profoundly dysfunctional household and in institutions with other troubled boys (and possibly even more troubled staff). But she always took pains to explain things to me and would ask me rather than order me to do things, which was another new experience and something to which I responded very well.

It was during those months that I decided I was going to be like my grandmother, Dr Margaret and Colonel Howard. It wasn't the Howards' trappings of money that appealed to me – the big house and the horses – it was the way they talked to each other and the 'smallness' of their behaviour in comparison to the melodramatic arguments and aggressive strife I'd been used to.

Gradually, fragments of the protective layer I'd built around myself fell away and, perhaps to everyone's surprise, including my own, underneath the sullen stubbornness and the don't-care facade was a little boy who was thoughtful and empathetic.

I'd been living with my grandmother for about eighteen months when everything changed abruptly. I knew her health hadn't been good, but I never discovered the reason why she told me, one sunny August morning, that I'd be leaving the cottage the following week and going to live in a local children's home. I was devastated. The world of a child is a small place and, like every child, I occupied a position at the centre of my world, which meant I related everything that happened in my life to my own actions. At the age of twelve, I could think of no explanation for being sent to a children's home other than that my grandmother didn't want me any more because I'd done something wrong. And maybe I had; although if that *was* the case, I have absolutely no memory of what it might have been.

When I left the cottage for the last time a week

later, my grandmother cried. I didn't see her again until my wife and I visited her in hospital some years later, a few days before she died. And I didn't ever see Dr Margaret again. I was hurt and bemused at the time and I don't understand their decision any better now, but I'll always be grateful to them all.

When I left the village – for the second time – I no longer believed that I was an imbecile or a cab horse, as Flossie used to tell me I was; nor was I the 'dirty little street urchin' Mr Harrison had tagged me at Tyndale House. When I'd arrived to live with my grandmother, I'd believed – if only subconsciously – the pattern of my life was already set and the future wasn't something to look forward to. By the time I left I'd been shown a different way of doing things and I had something to aspire to.

Within an hour of leaving the cottage, I was installed in my new home a few miles away. It was a mixed home this time, with about forty girls and boys between the ages of four and fifteen. Otherwise, it seemed pretty much like the other institutions I'd lived in. The master in charge of the home lived there with his wife and nine-year-old daughter, and there were three other members of staff who lived in, all of them women in their thirties, and all of them sensible, practical and not unkind.

I was already enjoying school, and after the move I continued to go to the same secondary school.

Over the next few months, I also learned to play lawn tennis and chess, had archery lessons, was taught to swim and became a bit of an ace at table tennis!

When I woke up on the morning of the second Sunday of my new life and found a grey jacket and a pair of long trousers on my bedside locker, I was delighted. In those days, it was common practice for boys to wear shorts until at least the age of eleven. They weren't the well-fitting shorts people wear today; they were baggy, shapeless, knee length and usually made of grey flannel. So it was every boy's ambition to wear long trousers like a man, and I couldn't believe I'd just been given the first pair I'd ever owned. Although I was disappointed to be told they must only be worn on Sundays, at least that meant there was something to look forward to on a day that consisted, as it had done at the other children's homes I'd lived in, of attending a church service in the morning, going back for Sunday school in the afternoon, and back again for another service in the evening.

During the week, all the boys from the home wore short trousers to school, and as we were the only boys of our age to do so, it had the effect of singling us out as being different. None of the other boys dared to tease us, however, because we stuck together like glue and they knew that if they upset one of us, they upset us all.

Some Sundays were special days at the home and when they occurred you could almost feel the excitement like static electricity in the air. When we got back from Sunday school in the afternoon, we'd all run upstairs to splash water on our faces, comb our hair and polish the toes of our Sunday shoes on the backs of our socks. When we came down again, a member of staff would stand at the open door of the common room while we filed in. Occasionally, she'd pull one of the children out of the line and send them back upstairs to have another attempt at smartening themselves up. She didn't have to do that very often though, because we were keen to look our best.

Chairs would have been arranged in a neat line against each of the two longest walls of the common room, and we'd fall over each other in our eagerness to sit down – girls on one side, boys facing them on the other. And then the visitors would start to arrive.

Most of the people who came into the room had the same bright smiles on their faces, as if they were nervous but pretending not to be. They were all couples; some of them had a child with them and some were on their own. They'd walk down the two lines of seated children looking at each one as if they were examining horses at a market, which I suppose in effect is what they were doing, because they were all there for the same reason: they were looking for a child to adopt. The visitors barely even glanced at the older children; almost invariably they took only the very young ones. But knowing that didn't prevent us all from feeling excited. Perhaps this time . . .

In fact, I wasn't being offered for adoption at all because, despite not wanting me himself, my father had refused to allow it. I still felt a sense of nervous anticipation during those visits though. Maybe I allowed myself to imagine that one Sunday a couple might come into the room, take one look at me and decide that *I* was the child for them and they were going to adopt, come what may. There's no harm in dreaming.

Whenever a child was selected for adoption at one of the Sunday sessions, we were all almost as excited as we would have been if we'd been the one who'd been chosen. I think it made us feel that we were part of a unified whole and, by choosing *one* of us, the couple had expressed their approval of us all. I suppose it's a similar principle to buying a lottery or raffle ticket, finding you're just one digit away from the winning number and believing you almost won: it makes you feel hopeful, however misplaced your optimism.

During the three years I lived at that children's home, I grew up. I don't think I ever considered running away. Maybe at least part of the reason why I felt more settled than I'd done at the other places I'd stayed in was because I knew by that time that life wasn't all bad and I wasn't totally unlovable, as I used to believe. When you know that, some things become easier to deal with.

Another reason was the fact that the home was run by people who had an understanding of children and who didn't rely on physical violence to keep them under control. I remember being very surprised to discover that almost every member of the staff had a sense of humour. The first time I became aware of it was shortly after I'd arrived, when one of them told me, 'If you ever want to run away, Peter, just let the master or one of the carers know, and we'll make you up a packed lunch to take with you.' It made me laugh when she said it, and after that, running away would have seemed like an over-reaction.

I'd been at the home for almost four months when Christmas came around. The previous Christmas, which I'd spent with my grandmother, had been the first one in my life I'd looked forward to. This was the second.

I knew the staff had planned a special meal for us and that after lunch we were going to play games, but I hadn't expected there to be presents. So when I woke up early on Christmas morning, went downstairs, opened the door of the common room and saw almost the entire floor covered with pillow-cases tied at the top with string and bursting at the seams with presents wrapped in brightly coloured paper, I couldn't believe my eyes. There was a label on every pillowcase and on every label there was a name. For some reason, I didn't think I'd find my own name, although that didn't stop me from look-ing. Other children had woken up by that time and the room soon reverberated with the sound of their excited voices as they read the labels and started tearing open their presents.

I was surprised when I found a pillowcase with a label that had my name on it. Instead of untying the string, I ran out of the room to look for a member of staff and almost collided with one of the women who'd just come down the stairs. She smiled at me and, raising her eyebrows in an expression of mock astonishment, said, 'Goodness, Peter! Where are you rushing off to in such a hurry?'

'There's a pillowcase,' I told her, and then, aban-doning any attempt to sound as if I didn't really mind one way or the other, 'There's a label with my name on it, but I don't know if it's really mine.'

The woman reached out her hand to push back a lock of hair that had fallen in front of my eyes and said, in a slow, thoughtful sort of voice, 'Hmm, well. I would say . . .' She paused and stroked her chin with her thumb and index finger as if she was considering an insoluble conundrum. 'I would saaay . . . if it has your name on it . . .' When she paused again, I think my whole body began to vibrate with barely contained excitement and she burst into laughter and added, quickly this time, 'I would say it was yours and you should definitely open it.'

If I'd been a cartoon character, I'd have left speed lines behind me as I shot back into the common room.

Adding up all the presents I'd been given throughout my entire life, the number wouldn't have come close to the number that were in that pillowcase. The best one of all was a wristwatch with luminous dial and hands, which came in a box that had the words 'To Peter, with love from Gran and Dr Margaret' written on it. For the rest of the day – and for days afterwards – I disappeared at intervals in search of a cupboard or some corner where I could look at my watch in the dark and marvel at the fact that I could tell the time even when I couldn't see my own hand held in front of my face.

That was a truly wonderful Christmas, and being given that watch did something remarkable to my sense of self-esteem, because I knew you wouldn't give a watch like that to someone who'd done something that had made you stop loving them.

Every week, we were given pocket money. I got two shillings, one shilling of which I had to save so

I'd have money to spend when we went on the annual summer holiday. Before going to live at the home, I hadn't ever been on a holiday, and going with lots of other children was really fun.

One year we went to Wales and visited an air show, where we watched in horror as a light aircraft spiralled out of the sky. By some miracle, it didn't crash into the crowd. Although I was upset because I knew I'd just witnessed the pilot's death, I felt a strange sense of elation too, because seeing things that were out of the ordinary made me feel that I was *living*.

During another summer we went to a small fishing village in Cornwall. I was fourteen and so was deemed old enough to go down to the harbour with some of the other boys without a member of staff. When we got there, we'd change into our swimming trunks and cheekily ask passing holidaymakers to throw coins in the deep water so we could dive in and retrieve them. On a hot sunny morning at the height of the holiday season, you could earn at least enough to buy an ice cream and a bag of chips.

One day while we were in Cornwall, we were all taken to see a pageant. I was standing a little distance away from the others, in the section that had been roped off for spectators, when my attention was caught by a man who was strolling past eating an ice cream. There was nothing unusual or striking about him and at first I didn't know why I'd noticed him, except that he looked vaguely familiar. Then I realized it was my father. I felt as if I'd been kicked in the stomach. Before I could stop myself, I'd reached out my hand to touch his arm.

When he turned to look at me, it was obvious he recognized me immediately, even though I must have grown – and grown up – quite a lot since he'd last seen me.

'What the bloody hell are you doing here?' he demanded, clearly not delighted by our extraordinary chance encounter. For a moment, I couldn't think what the bloody hell I *was* doing there, so instead of answering his question, I just stood staring at him like the imbecile he'd apparently always believed me to be.

All the staff at the home had come with us on the holiday and it was one of the women who came to my rescue. Appearing beside me out of the crowd, she smiled at my father, a cold, don't-mess-with-me smile, and asked, 'Are you all right, Peter? Do you know this man?'

I could feel a blush of embarrassment spread across my face. 'He's my father,' I said in a mumbled whisper.

The relationship obviously cut no ice with the woman, who nodded brusquely at my father and then put her hand on my arm as she said, 'Well, come along now, Peter. Let's get back to the others.'

I was turning away from my father to go with her when he called out, 'Wait. Wait a minute.' He put his hand into his pocket, pulled out two half-crowns and thrust them at me. I was still bemused and stupefied and when I didn't take the coins, the woman reached out her hand for them instead, thanked my father politely and then put her other hand under my elbow and steered me away. When I turned to look back, my father had already disappeared amongst the spectators. He must have been as shocked as I was by our meeting and perhaps he'd reacted out of guilt or embarrassment when he gave me that money. It was the first time in my life he'd ever given me anything. And it was to be the last.

On the whole, the children's home wasn't a bad place to live. Few things are 100 per cent good, however, and the rules were strict and not always fair. For example, if you arrived late for a meal or with dirty hands, you didn't eat, and every meal ended as soon as the master and staff had finished eating: anything that remained on your plate was taken away and served up to you again at the next meal, cold, congealed and disgusting. You got used to things like that though, and I suppose it did encourage us to be prompt and to eat up quickly.

Rather more serious than the petty rules of the dining room were the canings. If a boy or girl misbehaved, they were called to the master's study, where they had to take down their trousers or lift up their skirt and bend over the desk while they were given six of the best – which always struck me as an odd way to refer to beating a child with a wooden cane.

And then there were the things that happened that someone really should have put a stop to.

Chapter 10

Two evenings a week were designated bath nights, which were always organized and overseen by the master. With some forty children to wash and get ready for bed, the process took at least a couple of hours, even though we bathed two to a tub.

The master would choose two children at a time – always one boy and one girl – and they'd follow him upstairs to the bathroom, take off their clothes and climb into the bath, sitting at opposite ends facing each other. Seated on a small wooden chair, or sometimes on the toilet seat, the master would watch them as they washed, got out of the bath, dried themselves and put on their pyjamas. When those two children were ready for bed, he'd go downstairs again and select another boy and girl.

It was an embarrassing, humiliating ritual and a very strange way of doing things, particularly considering the fact that more than 50 per cent of the children at the school were aged between twelve and fifteen. But that was the way it was done, and refusing to comply would have made you look like a trouble-maker. We may not have liked it, but we accepted it as normal – or, at least, as being normal in the world we lived in. In fact, we never talked about it at all, even to each other. If we'd complained, who would have listened to a child who'd already been labelled 'disturbed'? Then, one day, something happened that made me abandon my usual determination to keep quiet and stay out of trouble.

There were three sisters who lived at the home: Mary, who was about thirteen; Brenda, who was eleven; and Bridget, who was seven. I'd noticed, as I think all the other children had done, that the master sometimes called Bridget to his office and when she came out again, she'd either be on the verge of tears or crying openly. Mary and Brenda always rushed to comfort her, but if you asked them what was wrong, they'd wave you away and say, 'Nothing. It's okay. It doesn't matter.' We didn't ever push them for an explanation: we were all children who'd been dumped by our parents or taken away from our homes for some reason and we understood the secrecy of self-protection. It was never a good idea to parade your weaknesses in front of the other children, even the ones who were your friends.

I was naive and far from worldly-wise and I didn't have a clue about what might be happening to make Bridget so upset. I was pretty certain she wasn't getting into trouble for something she'd done because she was a quiet, timid child who did what she was told and never answered back.

One of the leisure activities that took place at the home on Saturday afternoons was making wool rugs for people in the village. One Saturday when I was in the common room working on a rug with Mary and Bridget, the master came in and told Bridget he wanted to see her. I glanced across the table at her and was shocked by the fear I could see in her eyes and the expression of abject misery on her face. When the master called her again, impatiently this time, she gripped the edge of the rug and burst into tears.

'Bridget!' the master snapped at her for the third time. 'What's the matter with you, child? Leave what you're doing and come with me. Now!'

Bridget still didn't move, but as soon as the master took the first step across the room towards her I jumped off my stool. I'd acted instinctively and when he grasped her arm and began to try to pull her off her stool, I stood behind her, wrapped my arms around her thin little body and pressed her against the work table.

The master narrowed his eyes and glared at me as he demanded, 'Let her go, boy. Don't be ridiculous. Let go of her this minute!'

I didn't say anything at all; I just tightened my grip on Bridget and held my ground.

I was probably below average size for a boy of my age, and the master was quite a big man, but when he tugged at my arm and tried to pull me off her, determination gave me strength I didn't know I had. Surprised at my resistance, he let go of me for a second and I quickly slid my hand under the table and held on to the wooden ledge that ran round it. With the other hand, I gripped the rug, effectively wrapping it round Bridget's body like a net. At that moment, I'd have died rather than let go of her.

Unable to contain his fury at my disobedience and total disregard for his authority, the master started punching me on the back and shouting at me to let her go. When that didn't work, he caught hold of the tip of my ear and twisted it as hard as he could. But still I didn't release my grip on her. Suddenly, the words my brother had said to my father one day when we were living in Kent came into my head and I shouted at the master, 'If you don't leave her alone, I'm going to tell the police.' As I didn't know what happened in the master's office to make Bridget cry, I had no idea *what* I'd have told them, so I can't imagine what I'd have done if he'd called my bluff. Fortunately though, he didn't. With my words still hanging in the air like swords waiting to fall, the master turned on his heels and walked out of the common room, slamming the door behind him.

Within minutes, word had spread around the

home, and Brenda came running in from outside to comfort her sister and thank me for what I'd done.

There were no repercussions, as I'd felt sure there would be. In fact the master acted as though nothing had occurred at all, except that, as far as I'm aware, he never again called Bridget into his office. Bridget adopted me as her big brother and followed me whenever she could, like a shy little shadow. And I felt a sense of pride because I knew I'd done the right thing.

During my third year at the home, I had an unexpected visitor – my father's sister, Eileen. Eileen had married a man who worked for a major airline and they lived with their two children in a large house in Surrey. She was a kind, gentle woman. I think she'd refused to have anything to do with my father – from whom she was as different as chalk is from cheese – and I didn't have any memory of ever having met her before that day. I don't know why she came to see me; perhaps it was as a favour to my grandmother.

She suggested we should go for a walk together in the grounds of the home, and while we did so, we talked about everything under the sun. The only thing Eileen didn't talk about was my father. I did ask some questions about him, but instead of answering them, she shrugged her shoulders and changed the subject.

There was just one thing about Eileen's visit that I was later to regret: I'd never smoked a cigarette until she gave me one that day, and it started a habit I'm still struggling to break. When she took out a packet of Du Maurier cigarettes and lit one for herself from the flame of a very expensive-looking gold lighter, I was impressed. She offered one to me and I said, 'No thank you', not for any health-related reason, but because I was afraid a member of the staff might see me and then I'd get into trouble – which shows just how much of a hardened delinquent I really was!

However, curiosity – and perhaps a desire to look as sophisticated as I thought my aunt looked – made me succumb when she offered me one again a little while later. She laughed when the first drag made me cough until tears were streaming down my cheeks. But I persevered, and began to feel like one of the in-crowd.

Before she left that day, my aunt wrote her address and phone number on a piece of paper and gave it to me 'in case you ever need it'. In fact, I didn't see her again for more than thirty years, although I did speak to her on the phone a few years after that first meeting. It was a phone call I was to regret.

One hot, brilliant summer's day shortly after Eileen's visit, I was playing lawn tennis in the garden with one of the other boys and two of the carers when we heard a very loud popping noise, unlike anything I'd ever heard before. We all stopped playing and looked up into the sky and there, above our heads, were two airplanes. One of them, a Gloster Javelin with its distinctive T-tail and triangular wings, was flying low in the sky towards the hills, where we found out later it crashed into a picnic party, leaving no survivors. The other plane, a Hawker Hunter jet fighter, was spiralling out of the sky with its engines screaming.

One of the carers kept saying, 'Oh my God, oh my God,' very quietly, as if she was talking to herself. Then she gasped, as we all did when we realized that what looked like two puffs of smoke being blown out of the Hunter's cockpit were actually the pilot and navigator ejecting from the plane just seconds before it hit the ground above the village.

I shouted to the other boy to go with me and we raced out on to the lane and up the hill to the crash site, which was near a farm building at the edge of the village. An old air-raid siren was already sounding by the time we got close to the huge plume of black smoke that marked the place where the plane had hit the ground. There were bits of twisted metal everywhere and my friend and I just had time to snatch up a piece each before the army and police arrived. When we got back to the home and showed the other children our souvenirs, we were the envy of them all, and we felt like heroes.

The three years I lived at that home weren't bad years, all things considered. In fact, compared to the time I'd spent with Flossie and my father, they were pretty good. However, by the time I was fifteen – which was old enough to get a job – I was itching to move on, take control of my own life and start thinking about my future.

If I'd listened carefully enough, I'd probably have heard the distant echo of Fate's mocking laugh.

I can't remember what arrangements had been made for me before I left the children's home, but jobs were easy to find at that time, and I was excited about what lay ahead. One morning a couple of weeks before I was due to leave, I was summoned to the master's office and introduced to a man called Mr Gibson, who was a thin, balding man in a creased grey suit.

'Your father and stepmother want you to go home and live with them,' Mr Gibson told me, smiling and apparently oblivious to the fact that his words had hit me like a devastating blow. I didn't hear what else he said because my head seemed suddenly to be full of something that was preventing the sound of his voice passing from my ears to my brain. Mr Gibson probably thought Flossie and my father were doing me a huge favour by allowing me to go home again, particularly because the way I was staring at him in open-mouthed horror could have led him to believe that I was half-witted, at best.

When I tuned in again, he was saying, 'And, of course, as far as the law is concerned, you're too young to make your own decisions about things like this. So I'm sure it will all work out splendidly.'

There were all sorts of ways it might work out, but I knew that splendidly wasn't one of them.

I understood immediately what was behind my father and stepmother's apparent desire to have me at home after all these years: having got rid of me when I was young by making me the responsibility of the state – financially as well as in every other way – they'd decided to have me back now that I was going to be earning a wage.

Although I couldn't bear the thought of living with them again, I'd spent enough time in children's homes to know an irreversible decision when I was presented with one, and I knew there wasn't anything I could do or say that would make any difference.

Two weeks later, Mr Gibson returned to drive me to an estate in the suburbs of Cheltenham where Flossie and my father now lived. In fact, Mr Gibson was a nice man, and I realized during the journey I made with him that day that he wasn't really happy about what he was doing; but it was his job and he had no choice.

Saying goodbye to everyone and leaving the children's home for the last time proved to be even more difficult than I'd thought it would be. Not only was I leaving a place where I had friends and felt safe, I was going somewhere that held only bad memories for me and where no one liked me. Old habits die hard and it did cross my mind to run away, but I'd learned a great deal during the last three years and I knew that doing so would put me in the wrong and wouldn't really solve anything. So I sat beside Mr Gibson in his car, feeling sick and wishing I could believe him when he told me, 'It'll be all right, Peter. Don't you worry, lad. It'll all turn out all right.' I knew he wanted to cheer me up, but even without knowing Flossie and my father, he didn't sound convinced.

When we reached the outskirts of Cheltenham, I could feel my nerves and a resentful frustration building up inside me. I had to force myself to breathe evenly. If I arrived at the house all guns blazing, I was the only one who'd suffer for it. So it was better to accept the inevitable and try to make the best of it.

By the time we turned off the main road into an estate of new houses and stopped outside a bungalow, I was feeling profoundly miserable. As I got out of the car, I took a deep breath, squared my shoulders and straightened my back in an attempt to appear more confident than I actually was. I was fifteen and I'd just begun to feel some of the self-assurance that a young man *should* feel. Now, though, I was instantly transformed into my father's child again. The same sense of fear I used to have when I lived with him and Flossie had returned as if it had never gone away.

I was following Mr Gibson up the path from the pavement when the front door opened and my father stepped out, with Flossie just behind him. As soon as I saw them, all the old anxiety came flooding back and I had to clench my fists and clamp my teeth together until my jaw ached to stop myself shaking.

In fact, the first thing that struck me about them was how much older, smaller and less menacing they looked than the images I'd kept of them in my head. I suppose a few inches added to my own height and a few years to my age had changed my perspective. If I hadn't known better, I'd have thought their personalities had changed too, because they came bustling out of the house all cheerful friendliness, as if they were eager to welcome home the prodigal son. There was no reflection of their smiles in the cold expression in their eyes though.

'Come in, come in,' Flossie cooed in a voice that made her sound like a parody of the evil witch in a fairytale pretending to be a loving stepmother. She called me 'dear' and exclaimed about how much I'd grown since she'd last seen me – apparently oblivious to the irony of the fact that she was at least partly to blame for my having lived for the last few years in children's homes.

When she ushered us into the living room, I came face to face with the little queen – now considerably less little than she had been when I saw her last. My half-sister and I looked at each other and neither of us spoke.

While Flossie made us all a 'nice cup of tea', Mr Gibson explained to my father the terms of what he called 'the contract', the most important one of which, as far as I was concerned, was that when I found a job, I was to retain from my wages a minimum of ten shillings a week. The rest of my weekly pay packet would go towards my board and lodging, Mr Gibson said, but at least ten shillings *must* be mine to spend on whatever I wanted to spend it on.

'Of course!' My father nodded his head vigorously, as if shocked to the core by the very idea that he'd do anything other than what was fair and reasonable. Mr Gibson smiled at me, satisfied with the assurance he'd been given and clearly never having dealt before with people like my father and Flossie, who oozed sincerity and lied almost every time they opened their mouths.

When Mr Gibson had drunk his cup of tea, he shook my hand and wished me luck in my new life. I could see that he honestly believed the right decision had been made for me after all and he was leaving me in the best place. I wasn't fooled for a minute, and I was right not to be. As soon as the front door had closed behind him, Flossie and my father reverted to treating me with cold indifference.

My brother, sisters and stepbrothers no longer lived at home, and as the bungalow had three bedrooms, I had my own room, which is where I spent most of my time. There was an uncomfortable atmosphere in the house, as if dissatisfaction and bad temper had seeped into the air like a gas. It was worst at mealtimes, when little was said by anyone and anything that *was* said was irritably critical. To my surprise, however, none of it bothered me as much as I'd thought it would and although I felt wary and unsettled, I wasn't afraid, like I used to be.

My brother was married and living in another bungalow on the same estate, but he never came to see me while I was there, and I didn't visit him either. There was no bond between us at all, so I suppose neither of us was interested in making the effort. Perhaps part of the reason he kept away was because our father owed him money. Apparently my brother had lent him quite a considerable sum and had had to resort to the courts to get it back – even then, my father was repaying it at the rate of only one pound a week.

It seemed that the years had done nothing to redress my father's total lack of integrity, because he'd also borrowed money – and a cement mixer – from a man who was both a neighbour and a work colleague. It was only after my father had used the money as a deposit to buy the bungalow, done the job he'd wanted to do and sold the cement mixer that the poor neighbour learned never to believe any of his sob stories and never, ever, to 'lend' him anything.

The day after Mr Gibson had driven me to Cheltenham to reunite me with my loving family was a Saturday – a working day like any other at that time – and I was standing outside the labour exchange with my father before it had even opened. A little while later, we were at the counter, being questioned by the man whose job it was to find a job for me.

'Is he tough?' he asked my father, as if I was either invisible or too stupid to be able to answer for myself.

'He's as hard as bloody nails,' my father answered, which was a particularly strange thing to say when he didn't know anything about me at all. It was an answer that seemed to satisfy the man, however, and with one flourish of his pen I became a fully fledged member of the working class.

I started work on the Monday as a blacksmith's apprentice at a firm in Cheltenham called R. E. & C. Marshall. Even though my father told me nastily, 'You'll only be sweeping floors,' I was so excited to be starting work that I arrived at the forge early. And as it turned out, my father was wrong: instead of being handed a broom and told to get sweeping, I was given a pair of navy-blue overalls and shown how to pump the bellows that supplied the air that enabled the steel to get hot enough to be worked.

I soon understood why we had to wear overalls: the air in the forge was full of soot and metal scale, and by the time the hooter sounded for the first tea break at ten o'clock, I was covered in grime and soaked in sweat. It felt fantastic. While I was pumping the bellows, everything that had ever happened to me was forgotten and I was nothing more or less than a working apprentice. Until that moment, every aspect of my life had been moulded by other people; now it was my turn to take charge of my own destiny. I was earning money and I believed that if I worked hard, I could do anything I wanted.

It was while I was working at the forge that I discovered I had an ability to absorb vast amounts of information about things that interested me. Over the weeks that followed I learned a great deal, including how different levels of carbon make steel either hard or malleable; how to heat the metal to just the right temperature to be worked and then plunge it into warm water; and how, if the water's cold, hairline cracks can appear and weaken the whole structure as it hardens.

I was fascinated by the anvil and by the skill of the blacksmith, who used a hammer to beat red-hot steel into scrolls of different shapes and sizes. I'd noticed the blacksmith sometimes brought the hammer down on the anvil instead of on to the piece of steel he was beating, and when I asked him why he did it, he handed the hammer to me and told me to have a go. After I'd struck the steel a few times, with an enthusiasm that far outweighed my skill, the hammer began to slide out of my hand, and when I tapped it on the anvil – hard metal on hard metal – it sprang up again.

'Now loosen your grip,' the blacksmith shouted at me above the roar of the forge. 'Let the hammer slip back into your hand. See? Can you feel that? Now you're ready to go again.'

The men who worked at the forge were friendly and encouraging, particularly when they realized how interested I was in what they were doing and that, as well as being eager to learn from them, I was ready and willing to work hard. For someone like me who'd spent a good deal of his life up to that point believing he was stupid, the realization that I learned quickly and could carry out quite complicated tasks after only minimal instruction boosted my confidence and made me feel hopeful for my future.

When the time came for us to clock off at the end of the day, I was exhausted but happy.

'You can't clock off till you've urinated in the bucket,' one of the men told me as I was peeling off my filthy overalls and getting ready to go home. 'You have to rinse your hands in the urine and then wash them. It's a good idea to keep your mouth shut when you do that bit. Come on, lad. We all have to do it.'

The men laughed and I could feel myself blushing. I just hoped they played the same joke on all new apprentices and that it wasn't something they'd dreamed up for me because they thought I was stupid. In fact, it turned out that it wasn't a joke at all. It really was something they all did before they clocked off every day, because the ammonia in their urine helped to toughen the skin on their hands. I imagine forge workers today have found another way of doing that!

When I got home from work that day and at the end of each day that followed, no one asked me any questions about what I'd done. We ate our meal in silence and then I went to my room. It didn't matter though, because I'd worked hard and I was tired. I was enjoying the job at the forge and my confidence was boosted when the boss told me he was very pleased with my work.

When I woke up on the Friday morning at the end of the first week, I lay on my back in bed for a moment, looking up at the ceiling and trying to think why I felt so cheerful. Then I remembered: it was my first-ever payday.

It was quite late in the day when the woman from the office came into the forge carrying a small box. Although I pretended not to notice her, I watched surreptitiously as she handed out brown envelopes to all the men. At last she held one out to me and it was only when she laughed and patted my shoulder that I realized I was grinning from ear to ear. I blushed with pride when one of the men slapped me on the back and said, 'You worked hard for that, lad. You've earned it.'

There was still work to be done that day, and it wasn't until we had a brief break that I was able to pull the envelope out of my pocket, open it and count my earnings: three pounds ten shillings. When I got back to the bungalow that night, my father held out his hand without saying a word and I put the envelope on his upturned palm. In fact, I gave it to him gladly because the knowledge that I was paying for my board and lodgings made me feel I wasn't beholden to him or Flossie in any way and that I owed them nothing.

I stood there, waiting for my father to hand some money back to me, as had been agreed with Mr Gibson, but he just glared at me and said, irritably, 'What?'

'My ten shillings,' I answered. Suddenly, all my

confidence and pride evaporated and I felt like a stupid little boy again, because I'd believed my father would keep his word.

'Oh, yeah, well, I can't afford to give you anything right now,' he said, folding the notes and putting them in his pocket. 'Things are a bit difficult just now and I need all of it.'

I felt such a powerful sense of disappointment and frustration that I thought for one awful moment I was going to burst into tears. 'I can't afford to give you anything,' he'd said. He was talking about the money *I'd* earned. How could I have been so gullible as to believe he'd changed? Of course he hadn't: he was still the nasty, bullying con man he'd always been and always would be.

'Don't worry though,' he added, nodding his head as if to give credence to what he was saying. 'I'll give it to you next week. I promise.'

My distress had quickly turned to angry resentment and I was on the verge of losing my temper. It crossed my mind to punch him and take from him by force what was rightfully mine. Fortunately though, I didn't: hitting him might have given me a brief sense of satisfaction, but I knew I'd be the one to suffer in the long run as the result of any confrontation.

He didn't keep his promise the following week, or on any of the weeks that came after it. I suppose I could have taken my ten shillings out of the envelope before I gave it to him, but I didn't do that either, because I knew that even though I'd be taking what was rightfully mine, it would result in all hell breaking loose. By the end of a month, however, I'd formulated a plan.

Chapter 11

Although we were paid on Fridays, Saturday was also a normal working day. After I'd been at the forge for about five weeks, I came home on the Friday and told my father something had happened at work and we weren't going to be paid until the following morning. My heart was thumping when I said it, but, fortunately, he was too certain of his control over me to doubt what I told him – after all, he'd been taking every penny I'd earned for more than a month without my ever having put up any resistance.

The next morning, I ate a good breakfast and left the house for work at the usual time. But instead of walking to the forge, I continued on along the road to St James railway station and, using one pound ten shillings of the money I'd been paid as normal the previous day, bought a single train ticket to London.

The train to Paddington wasn't due to leave until late afternoon, which meant I had to find something to do for the rest of the day. Knowing I wasn't safe as long as I was still in Cheltenham, I spent the next few anxious hours walking round the town looking in shop windows and sitting on a bench in the park watching the ducks on the pond.

I wanted to buy a packet of cigarettes. As I hadn't had any money before then, I hadn't been able to buy any for weeks, and I thought smoking might make me look calm and relaxed, like someone who knew what he was doing and had every right to do it, rather than like the fugitive I really was. However, after buying my ticket, I had only two pounds left in the brown envelope, and because I didn't know what was going to happen when I arrived in London, I didn't dare spend it. Despite having confidence born of total ignorance about the certainty of being able to find a job as soon as I got off the train, I didn't know how long the two pounds would have to last.

In the afternoon, I returned to the railway station, found the platform for the train to London, and sat in the almost empty waiting room, wishing I was already on my way. I still had the lunch I'd taken with me from the house that morning, as I did every day when I went to work. I didn't know when I'd next get something to eat, so I'd planned to keep it for as long as possible. Suddenly, that morning's breakfast seemed a very long time ago, and I unwrapped my sandwiches and ate some of them.

As the time approached when I'd normally be due home from work, the apprehension I'd been feeling all day reached new heights. At the end of the working day, a few other people came into the waiting room and I decided to stand outside. I'd almost convinced myself that I was on the wrong platform when there was a loud crackling noise followed by a nasal voice which echoed from the vaulted ceiling above me as it announced that the next train due to arrive on the platform on which I was standing would be the train to Paddington, London.

By the time the train pulled into the station amidst a flurry of whistling, clanging steam, I was so jumpy with nerves that when a man glanced towards me and raised his hand, I was certain he was about to point at me and shout, 'There he is! That's the boy who's run away!' And then the next minute, the doors of the train were being flung noisily open and I was propelled forward into a carriage by the people behind me on the platform. I sat down in a window seat facing the engine, turned my back to the glass and hunched my shoulders: there was still time for my father to come striding through the station looking for me.

I heard the three young women long before they burst through the door of the compartment I was sitting in. They were still laughing and chattering as they threw themselves down on seats at the other end of it, and they talked all the way to London, which I found somehow comforting, perhaps because the fact that they considered their journey to be mundane and ordinary made me feel a little less daunted by it. I still wished I had a packet of Du Maurier cigarettes though.

Just as I was imagining Flossie and my father running into the station, followed closely by policemen waving handcuffs above their heads, the guard blew his whistle. There was a sound like rapid gun shots as the doors slammed shut along the length of the platform, a great hiss of steam, the scraping of metal on metal, and the train started to move.

As it drew out of the station and began to speed through the gathering darkness, I thought about what I'd just done. I was sorry to have left my job at the forge, particularly after having been there for such a short time. By leaving so abruptly, I felt I'd let down the people who'd trusted me and given me a sense of pride in my own abilities. But I knew that if I'd stayed, my father would have continued to take all the money I earned, until eventually I'd have been forced into some sort of confrontation with him. I wasn't really afraid of my father any more – well, perhaps I was a bit. What I *was* afraid of, however, was doing something that would get me into trouble. So I was running away – again. I just hoped this time I wasn't going to have to sleep in a cowshed or in a den in the woods.

Thinking about the fact that I was running away made me suddenly wonder if I *looked* like a runaway, in my scuffed black shoes, short, shapeless grey trousers and crumpled jacket, which was a size too small for me and the sleeves of which didn't reach my wrists. I glanced quickly towards the young women. How must I look to them? Probably like a scruffy schoolboy on his way home at the end of the day, although it was more likely they hadn't thought about it at all. In fact, they seemed to have forgotten there was anyone else in the carriage with them.

The farther away the train took me from Cheltenham, the more easily I breathed, except when we stopped at other railway stations, when I shrank back into my seat and turned my face away from the window. I was excited about going to London, but I was nervous too. At one point, I closed my eyes with the idea of getting some sleep before I arrived, and then opened them again almost immediately when a multitude of thoughts and questions started tumbling around in my head. As a very young child, I'd survived many nights sleeping outside in the cold and rain and, one way and another, I'd had plenty of practice adapting to new situations. So, whatever happened in London, I told myself, it wouldn't be any worse than the things I'd already had to deal with.

When the train began to slow down and the fields gave way to rows of houses on either side of the railway track, I glanced down at the watch my grandmother and Dr Margaret had given me as a present one Christmas that now seemed a lifetime ago. It was almost half past nine. The train moved over some points as it changed from one track to another and the sound it made was like words, which I kept repeating in my head: not going back, clickety clack, not going back.

The three girls stood up and lifted their bags from the overhead shelf, while I looked out of the window at the steadily falling rain illuminated in the yellow glow of the lamp posts on the streets, and tried to swallow the lump that had suddenly developed in my throat. It would have been nice to know that I had somewhere warm and safe to sleep that night, as the girls clearly had. But there was nothing to be gained from feeling sorry for myself. I'd made a decision and now I was going to have to see it through and make the best of it.

When the train stopped at Paddington Station, the girls glanced towards me and smiled before leaving the compartment to join the flow of people already hurrying along the platform. After they'd gone, I continued to sit there for a few moments, staring out through the window beside me and wishing someone was coming to meet me.

Eventually, I stood up, took a deep breath and stepped down on to the platform. In those days of steam trains, the billowing smoke, sounds and smells that accompanied every arrival and departure made each journey seem like an adventure. On this occasion, however, any excitement I might have felt was almost completely swamped by anxious trepidation. With its high, glazed roof and wrought-iron arches, the station itself was impressive and before I'd even stepped out into the city, I had a sense of being someone very small somewhere very big.

Having gone to the cinema with my class at school to see the film *Reach for the Sky* – about the RAF pilot and Second World War hero Douglas Bader – I thought I had at least some idea of what London was like. I was wrong! Films in those days were in black and white, but the road outside the station was in glorious Technicolor. There were bright-red double-decker buses, black taxi cabs, cars, people hurrying along the pavements or weaving in and out of the traffic as they crossed the road, and noise. It seemed that everyone, except me, knew where they were going and wanted to waste no time getting there.

I stood for a moment, breathing in the smell of the city and listening to its sounds, and then I turned and went back into the station. As I'd been walking towards the exit, I'd noticed a small shop on the concourse selling cigarettes, and I really needed something to steady my nerves. I didn't dare spend what it cost to buy a pack of Du Maurier, so I bought the cheapest cigarettes – ten untipped Woodbines – and a box of matches.

Standing just outside the station again, I opened the packet, lit a cigarette and took a long drag. The coughing fit that overcame me and, when I could breathe again, the feeling that I was going to faint – at the entrance to Paddington Station, within minutes of arriving in London to start my new life – rather ruined my plan of appearing sophisticated and nonchalant. My already barely discernible self-assurance was damaged further when I only narrowly avoided being hit by a speeding black cab as I crossed the road.

I'd walked only a few yards in a randomly selected direction when I saw above the doorway of a tall terraced house a large, white, oval sign with the words 'Forty Nine Hotel' written on it in red lettering. The lights shining from the windows of the building made it look warm and inviting. It had started to rain and suddenly I felt very tired and cold. I crossed the road, stood at the foot of the stone steps that led up from the pavement to the front door, and wondered whether I was doing the right thing. There was only one way to find out, and, after all, I wasn't exactly spoilt for choice: at that moment, my list of options began and ended with the Forty Nine Hotel.

I straightened my back and then walked up the steps and rang the bell.

The young woman who opened the door was

pretty and her smile was friendly. Although I desperately wanted to give the impression that I was the sort of person who often stayed in hotels, I don't think worldly-wise and confident were the words that sprang immediately to her mind when she saw me standing on the doorstep with a steady stream of water dripping off my thick curly hair and down my neck. I could see her taking it all in, but she didn't give any sign of what she was thinking. She just asked, politely, 'Can I help you?'

'I'm . . . I'm looking for a place to stay,' I answered, cursing myself silently for stuttering like a fool, and then adding quickly, 'I'm going to find work on Monday.'

'Well that's grand!' the young woman said. 'And you've come to the right place – I mean, if you're looking for somewhere to stay.' She smiled again and then she opened the door wide, stepped back into the brightly lit hallway and said, 'You better come in out of the rain.'

She was closing the door behind me when another, older woman walked into the hall through a doorway on the right.

'We have a guest, Mother,' the young woman said. 'He's going to get a job on Monday and he needs somewhere to stay.'

It must have been obvious to them both that I wasn't the normal sort of hotel guest – for a start,

I had no luggage – but they couldn't have been nicer to me. I was very lucky to have ended up on the doorstep of the Forty Nine Hotel in Norfolk Square, although it wasn't until some time later when I found out what a dangerous place London could be for the naive and unwary that I understood just how lucky I'd actually been.

'It's three pounds ten shillings a week for bed and breakfast,' the older woman told me.

I felt in my pocket for the now-soggy brown envelope and began to count out the money I had left. 'I did have two pounds,' I told the woman, 'but I bought some cigarettes and now I . . .'

'Oh, don't you worry about that, love.' The mother smiled as she interrupted me. 'It can wait till Monday, when you've found that job. Now, I expect you want to get to bed. Rita will show you your room.'

When Rita left me alone in a small room on the first floor, I drew the curtains to shut out the dismal night and sat down on the bed, and as I did so, I felt a huge weight of anxiety lifting off my shoulders. Suddenly, it seemed possible that everything might turn out well after all; and that's when I realized that until then I hadn't really believed it would.

I was still sitting on the bed going over the day's events in my head when there was a knock on the door. Instantly, my contentment turned to panic. I'd been discovered. Maybe Rita and her mother had known all along that I was a runaway and they'd only been pretending to be friendly and helpful until I was safely out of the way upstairs, when they'd phoned the police. With my heart racing, I opened the door just wide enough to see who was standing on the other side of it.

'We thought you might need something to eat and drink,' Rita said, in her cheerful, friendly voice. She held out a plate of sandwiches and a mug of something steaming and I could feel a hot blush of embarrassment suffuse my face. It was a good thing to be wary – I'd known since I was a very small boy that I couldn't ever allow my guard to slip completely – but it was an even better thing to know who I could trust. And I knew I shouldn't have doubted for one moment that the kindness of the two women was genuine. With a full stomach and a warm, comfortable bed, I slept well that night.

When I woke up at half past seven the next morning, it took me a few seconds to remember where I was. It was the first time I could remember waking up on a Sunday morning knowing that I could do whatever I wanted to do. Every Sunday when I'd been living at the children's homes, I'd had to go to church, and when I was in Cheltenham with Flossie and my father, I'd stay in my room or go out – anywhere – on Sundays just to get out of their way.

When Rita had led the way upstairs the previous

night, she'd opened the door to the left of mine to show me a small bathroom, which was shared by all the people with rooms on the first floor. I'd hung up my wet jacket, shirt and trousers to dry before I went to bed, and after I'd had a wash I put them on. Then I took the red-bound Bible out of the drawer in the little table beside the bed, lay down on my back and began to read it – just for something to do.

It was almost nine thirty when there was a gentle knock on my door. This time, I had no fear that it might be the police. In fact, it was Rita and her mother, who'd come to see how I was settling in. They told me the rules of the house – which, to someone who'd lived with Flossie and in children's homes for most of their life, didn't seem like rules at all. And then they showed me how to work the radio and intercom, which were fixed to the wall above the head of the bed.

'We use the intercom to wake up the guests who are going out to work,' Rita's mother said. 'So when you get that job tomorrow, you won't have to worry about getting up on time.' Her apparent assumption that I'd find a job the next day gave a much-needed boost to my morale.

The two women had only just left my room when there was another knock on the door. This time it was a Jamaican woman who'd come to see who'd moved into the room next to the one she lived in with her husband. She came back a little while later to invite me to Sunday lunch, which was every bit as good as the smells that had been wafting under my door. The Jamaican woman's husband was as nice and as friendly as she was, and so were the other hotel guests who came knocking on their door to meet 'the new arrival'.

When I went to bed that night, it felt as if I'd taken a huge leap off a very high cliff and, contrary to my true expectations, had landed firmly and safely on my feet. I couldn't wait to see what the next day would bring.

At seven thirty on Monday morning, I was woken up by the sound of a voice on the intercom. As soon as I was washed and dressed, I went downstairs to the dining room, where Rita and her mother were already serving breakfast. Before I left the house a little while later, I made a solemn vow to myself that I would not return until I'd found a job.

Having walked down Praed Street, I was on the Edgware Road when I saw a note in a shop window that said 'Assistant wanted'. It was a shop that sold televisions and radio sets, but as it was still early in the morning, it hadn't yet opened. The rush hour was in full swing, however, and as I continued on along the road, looking in every shop window for other cards advertising vacant positions, people were hurrying in every direction, on foot and in vehicles, on their way to work.

At precisely nine o'clock, I returned to 207 Edgware Road, opened the door of the shop and told the man behind the counter that I was looking for work. A few questions and answers later – one or two of the latter of which were necessarily ambiguous – I was taken on as the new assistant at the Premier Radio Company. My wages were to be five pounds a week; I would work all day Monday to Friday as well as Saturday mornings; and I would start the next day.

Despite assuring my new employer that my insurance card would be forwarded to me in the post from Cheltenham and that I'd bring it in as soon as it arrived, I had no idea what an insurance card was. Whatever it was, I was fairly certain I didn't have one. But I needed the job, so I just hoped that the incredible luck I'd had since I'd arrived in London would continue, and the problem would somehow solve itself.

I almost ran back to the hotel to tell my good news to Rita and her mother, who I now knew to be called Mrs Hardy. It was a nice feeling to have people to share it with, and they seemed almost as pleased by it as I was.

I couldn't wait for the morning to come so that I could start my job. I went out of the hotel again at lunchtime and bought some fish and chips, which I ate sitting on a bench in Norfolk Square. Then I wandered around the streets, trying to take everything in and feeling real excitement at last, knowing my new life was about to begin.

I thoroughly enjoyed working at the shop. One of my more mundane jobs was packing television components, although even that was interesting because I was learning how televisions worked. What really fascinated me were the crystal sets. As well as selling crystal sets ready to use, we sold them in kit form, and I was taught how to build a set and test it. Instead of being powered by mains electricity or batteries, as normal radio sets were, crystal sets were passive receivers of radio waves, which they picked up by means of a long antenna. They got their name from the detector they contained, which was made of a crystalline mineral called galena and which came into contact with a coil of copper wire when you turned the knob on the front of the set. As the radio signal was weak, you had to listen through headphones, which added to the sense that you were doing something scientific as well as fun.

Within days, I was happy at work and happy living at the hotel. After paying Mrs Hardy for my room every week, I still had one pound ten shillings left over, which was quite a reasonable amount of money in those days. I bought myself some clothes and had a haircut, although I was careful to put some money aside because I had to buy my supper every day – only breakfast was provided at the hotel. Usually, I'd get fish and chips or a steak and kidney pie with gravy, which I'd take back to eat in my room or, when the weather was fine, in the garden in the square. Sometimes my Jamaican neighbours invited me in for a meal, and I made other friends too, both at work and outside it, some of whom took me to see the sights of London.

I had a good, steady job and a nice place to live just a short walk away from the shop. I felt very pleased with myself, and very happy to have discovered that the world was a good place after all.

I think it was because I felt so proud of what I'd achieved within a few weeks of arriving in London with two pounds, half a sandwich and the clothes I stood up in, that I felt I wanted to share the news of my good fortune with someone. The trouble was, I couldn't think of a single person who'd be interested. Then I remembered my father's sister, Eileen, and how nice she'd been to me when she'd visited me at the children's home. I'd lost the piece of paper she'd given me, but I knew she lived in Richmond, in Surrey, and when I thought about it hard enough, I remembered the name of the road she lived in. So one day I went into a telephone box, looked up her name in a phone book and dialled her number.

My aunt was obviously surprised when she realized it was me. She listened as I told her all about my new life in London and how well I was doing, and I was pleased when she asked me questions about my job and about the hotel I was living in. At the end of the phone call, she wished me well, and when I put down the receiver I felt glad I'd phoned her.

As well as wanting to share my good news with someone, I think I also wanted a member of my family to know that I'd done well and that I wasn't an imbecile after all. Aunt Eileen was the only one I thought might be interested and happy for me. And she was the only one I thought I could trust.

Chapter 12

A few hours after I'd made the phone call to my aunt, I was sitting in the back of a police car on the way to the nearest police station.

I was devastated when two policemen arrived at the radio shop. I felt betrayed by my aunt and I had a sense of disappointment that was almost a physical pain. I don't know what I'd thought had happened when I'd disappeared that day from Cheltenham. I don't think I'd thought much about it at all once the train had started moving. I'd been afraid my father might come looking for me at the station if he found out I hadn't been at work that day, but once I got off the train in London, I thought I'd escaped, and it never even crossed my mind that I'd have been reported as missing. I believed Flossie and my father would be as happy to get rid of me as I was to get away from them.

I had no understanding of the tangled web that grows around a child once they've become the responsibility of the state, or of the fact that social services were bound to keep tabs on me until I was old enough to be legally independent. So I didn't realize that, however much he might have wanted to do so, my father couldn't just shrug his shoulders, think 'good riddance' and close the door behind me. So he'd reported me as missing – if only to cover his own back.

When my aunt put down the telephone receiver after talking to me, she picked it up again immediately and phoned my brother. Her questions and her interest in where I was working and living had been purely and simply for the purpose of discovering my whereabouts so she could tell my brother, who passed the information on to the police.

When the policemen came for me at work I was whisked away and didn't get a chance to say goodbye to Rita and her mother or to the friends I'd made among the other hotel guests. During the time I'd spent in London, I'd begun to trust people. It took just one phone call, made by my aunt, to bring the shutters crashing down again. I was angry with my brother too: he knew what my childhood had been like; he'd witnessed many, many times the physical expression of the animosity Flossie and our father felt towards me. Why hadn't he come to find me himself, to see how I was getting on and maybe make a brotherly judgement about whether being taken back to live in Cheltenham was really the best thing for me?

In fact, after the police picked me up that day, I

wasn't taken 'home' to Cheltenham. When I was interviewed at the police station, I told them about my father keeping all the money I'd earned when I was working at the forge. I insisted that if they did send me back, I'd simply run away again, and I'd keep running away until I was old enough not to require a legal guardian.

Maybe someone else had spoken to them already and they knew something of my background, or maybe they simply believed what I told them. They could certainly see that I was clean, neatly dressed and well fed, and that I'd been looking after myself more than adequately for the last few weeks. Whatever the reason, instead of being sent back to live with Flossie and my father, I was taken to a children's home in Leicester while the powers that be considered the options. I was heartbroken to be leaving London, but I was used to moving on and I knew, once again, that I didn't have any alternative.

I stayed at the home in Leicester for about a month. Oddly, although I can't remember anything about it at all, I do remember in detail the job I had while I was there, working at a clothing firm called Hart and Levy, making jackets. There was a sheet of tickets that went down the line with every jacket being made and as you completed your part of the process – in my case, merely pressing the inside shoulders with a large steam iron – you tore off a ticket from the sheet. At the end of the day, your tickets were counted and money was added to your weekly pay packet. The wages were good: each of my tickets was worth one shilling and nine pence and I was earning as much as eight pounds a week. But it wasn't London and I wasn't going back every evening to the Forty Nine Hotel.

Despite everything, I'm an optimist by nature. Sometimes, though, you encounter a cloud that doesn't seem to have even the smallest fragment of a silver lining. Being in London was like being shown something I'd always wanted that had turned out to be even better than I'd ever imagined it would be. But as I reached out my hand to grasp it, someone pulled me back and said, 'Sorry, we got it wrong. That's not for you after all; it belongs to someone else. *This* is yours.' And when they opened a door and showed me something nobody would ever want, I thought, 'Of course it is. I should have known.'

After a month, the people responsible for my well-being had had their discussions and made their decisions. I was accompanied on the train, which took me from Leicester to Bristol, from where I was driven by car to the National Nautical School near Portishead.

Opened in 1869 aboard the training ship *Formidable*, which was leased from the government by a group of Bristol businessmen and anchored some four hundred yards off the pier, the school was originally established with the aim of getting young 'urchins' off the Bristol streets and training them to be seamen. In 1906, after the ship was damaged in strong gales, three hundred and fifty orphans and court-sentenced urchins were moved into a huge new building overlooking the Bristol Channel, which is where I was taken that day.

I was fifteen years old when I arrived at the nautical school, and it was expected that I would remain there for at least two years.

Discipline at the school was strict and everything was based on Royal Navy principles. There were just one hundred and fifty boys by that time, from all over the country and from all types of background. Some couldn't read or write; some had been in street gangs and had few skills beyond fighting and handling knives; some were displaced, as I was; and some were just plain bad.

Like regular sailors, we wore caps with ribbon around the brim, had seven creases in each leg of our bell-bottom trousers, and were responsible for taking care of our own kit from bunk to bugle. Every cadet had to learn to play the bugle. We took it in turns to sound reveille at sunrise, the retreat call at sunset, and the last post on ceremonial occasions, and woe betide any boy who played a wrong note. Also, we all had to be able to climb up to the crow's nest sixty feet above the ground on the ship's mast that stood outside the school building facing the Bristol Channel.

Except for a civilian training officer and a female cook, every member of staff at the nautical school was ex-navy. First in command was Captain Campbell, who maintained control of the disparate bunch of boys under his care by enforcing rigid discipline. Below him were two commanders who taught us seamanship, and two other officers who took us for regular academic school lessons and sport. As well as being strict and exacting, the training staff were fair, and they must have been tough too, when you think that just six officers kept control of more than one hundred and fifty boys, who, particularly as new intakes, were mostly wayward, undisciplined and sometimes aggressive.

There were three divisions – Anson, Benbow and Hood – all named after ships and each one comprising fifty-two boys, whose conduct was the responsibility of the boys who had been appointed as leading hands. As with anything else, what happened within each division depended on the character of the boy in charge. I was put in Benbow Division and almost immediately had to face the first hurdle of initiation. It didn't take me long to realize that there were actually four boys who controlled what occurred in my division, all of them unpleasant, belligerent bullies who took it upon themselves to think up some potentially dangerous initiation tasks.

I was held out of a third-floor window in a mattress cover. Only a fool with no imagination wouldn't have been frightened, but I'd long ago perfected the art of not showing my fear, and after ten minutes they pulled me back into the room. Having passed the test, I thought the initiation process was over. The bullies weren't so easily satisfied, however, and my second test was to fight another boy. In fact, it was all over pretty quickly, both because I was determined not to show any sign of weakness and because the poor lad wasn't the fighting type. My reward was to be accepted as part of the bullies' gang. Although it was a dubious honour, I'd learned from my time living in children's homes that it was always better to be 'in' than 'out' – and I knew that we were all going to be there long enough for me to settle the score.

The first few months I spent at the nautical school were very tough. Gradually though, I began to get used to it and I found that the regularity of the life, as well as the discipline and the fact that I was learning something new every day, suited me well. I learned a great deal about seamanship – and I can still remember the names of all the countries in South America!

One of our regular tasks was testing the seaworthiness of the lifeboats carried by oil tankers and old coal boats that docked at Avonmouth. The problem was that the lifeboats we tested were never used from one year to the next, which meant that their timbers dried out and almost as soon as we started to row, we found ourselves up to our waists in water, barely able to move the oars at all. It was fun though, and it wasn't long before I'd decided that when the time came for me to leave the school, I wanted to join the merchant navy.

I wouldn't ever forgive my Aunt Eileen or my brother for sending the police after me when I was in London. But if they hadn't done so, I wouldn't have gone to Portishead, and then I wouldn't have learned all the things I learned while I was there.

After a year, I was made up to leading hand of Benbow Division, and I was immensely proud of the gold-anchor insignia that was added to the left arm of my uniform. Most of the bullies who'd been responsible for my initiation into the division had already left. They'd made many of the boys' lives extremely miserable, including my own from time to time; I was determined I wasn't going to be like them. Perhaps it was because the other boys were tired of being intimidated and oppressed that they responded as well as they did when I used reason instead of threats and bullying, and things began to change.

One day, I was sent for by the captain, who was

standing on the parade ground looking out across the water when I approached him and saluted smartly.

'I've been watching the boat you'll be sailing out on,' the captain told me. 'The SS *Hadriana*; she's a passenger cargo ship.' I looked in the direction he was indicating and saw what appeared to be a very old boat that was in desperate need of some maintenance work to make it seaworthy. She was the best boat I'd ever seen.

Of all the homes I'd lived in during the years of my childhood, the nautical school was the one I was most sorry to have to leave, even though doing so meant I would be free at last of my father and stepmother and of the state authorities that had taken over responsibility for me. I was excited too, because a different door had opened, allowing me to catch a glimpse of my future, which was potentially a far better future than any I might have imagined.

Ships only remain in dock for a couple of days, and the next morning, after I'd said goodbye to my friends and to the staff who'd dragged me, sometimes kicking and screaming, from childhood to become a man, I was driven down to Avonmouth dock. Before I could board the boat, I had to undergo an eye test and have my photograph taken for my merchant navy ID card. Later, as I walked up the gangway of the SS *Hadriana* carrying a suitcase full of good, sturdy clothes that would see me through the next few months, the butterflies were back. This time, though, I was excited and not frightened at all.

I was to be the *Hadriana*'s deck boy – the lowest rank on the boat – but I'd have gladly been the deck boy's assistant if that had been the only job available. I was allocated a bunk in the very small cabin I'd be sharing with four other sailors. As I went in to stow my suitcase, a sailor who was signing off the ship pointed to a guitar lying on one of the bunks and said, 'I don't need it any more. You can have it.' Working in a lowly position on a boat is hard graft, but you also spend many idle hours at sea and I filled a lot of them by teaching myself to play tunes on that guitar, which I kept for years.

When we set sail that evening, I stood on the stern end of the boat watching the sailors preparing to let go the ropes and listening to the engine splutter and rattle into life. And then I was violently sick.

'Bring it up, lad,' one of the sailors called across the deck to me. 'You never know: it might be a gold watch!' He laughed and slapped me on the back as he walked past where I was emptying the entire contents of my stomach over the side of the boat. The feeling that I was going to die lasted for several minutes and then never returned again, even in the stormiest of raging seas.

When my stomach was empty, I leaned over the

stern rail watching the lights along the coast flicker as we slowly steamed away from the land. I'd forgotten about my father and Flossie and about everything that had happened during my childhood. I wasn't anyone's son or brother or irksome responsibility; I was Peter Kilby, seventeen years old and a sailor, eager for adventure and on my way to Jamaica at the start of a brand new life.

After Jamaica it was Trinidad and from there I took a berth on another boat, an oil tanker this time, which was bound for Holland. From Holland, I went to Bombay (now Mumbai), through the Bay of Bengal and up the Hooghly River to the Port of Calcutta, across the Indian and South Atlantic oceans, through the Panama Canal to South America, and on around the world and across most of its seven seas.

As I gained experience as a sailor, I was promoted and I soon lost count of the number of countries I'd visited. I saw things I couldn't ever have imagined – sharks and giant manta rays in the Indian Ocean, the Northern Lights from a ship on the Lawrence River en route to Quebec City, and terrible things too. There were children with twisted, useless limbs who lined the docks in India begging for money with a hopeless, clamouring desperation that broke my heart. Seeing them there, dirty, emaciated, disabled and completely uncared for, made me realize how appalling children's lives can be when there's no real infrastructure – however imperfect – to catch them when they fall. The damage done to me when I was a child was largely psychological. By comparison to those children, I'd been lucky.

I was on an old tanker owned by Eagle Oil for almost a year. It was a tramp steamer, which meant the captain received orders for our next voyage when we arrived at each port, and the ship could be away from its home port for years as it transported oil from one country to another.

I'd been at sea for about two years when I returned to England, a much wiser and richer person than I'd been when I left. I didn't have a home to go back to, so I went to stay in the Cotswolds, which was the only area of the country I really knew. When I was shopping in a small town one day, I bumped into one of my sisters. I was surprised she recognized me at all: the last time she'd seen me, I'd been a thin, pallid little boy, and now I was a strong, sunburned young man. Perhaps it was the mop of unruly dark hair that identified me.

My sister invited me home to meet her husband and while I was there she managed to coax some money out of me to pay for a wooden fence she wanted to have put up round their garden. After I'd told them about some of my adventures at sea, my sister said, 'I suppose the merchant navy is all very well, but what you should do is join the army. In the army you could have a *real* career.' The way she talked about it did make it sound appealing, and within a week I'd signed off from my life at sea.

I did twelve-week basic training at Oswestry in Shropshire and then went to Aldershot for further training as a paratrooper. It was tough, but it was fun, and having spent a good deal of my early childhood as a loner, I enjoyed the camaraderie that existed among the soldiers. However, after eighteen months, I changed my mind about being a paratrooper, which was a decision that earned me twenty-eight days in 'The Glasshouse' at Colchester Barracks. When I'd served my time in detention, I was sent to an artillery unit in Colchester to await my discharge, which took six months to come through.

When I left the army, I returned once more to the Cotswolds, rented a flat in a small town and, after doing a short course, became a driving instructor for the British School of Motoring in Gloucester. I enjoyed the work, but it wasn't long before I began to suffer from a version of what we used to call when I was at sea 'the channels'. Sailors get the channels when they're approaching their home port (via the English Channel) and become restless and unable to settle to anything because they can't wait to see their families and friends. For me, it just meant itchy feet and a desire to move on.

When I left that first flat, I took lodgings in Cheltenham. It was while I was there that someone told me about a firm called Seismograph Service Limited, which had recently set up camp in the nearby village of Bishop's Cleave and was taking on drivers for its water tankers and Land Rovers. I caught a bus to Bishop's Cleave the next day and tracked down the company's temporary office in an old station yard.

The yard was littered with Land Rovers, water tankers and Thames Trader lorries, all of which were left-hand drive vehicles sporting a logo on the driver's door of a picture of the world as a globe overprinted with the letters SSL. There was also a caravan in the yard, which was being used as an office and recruitment centre. Inside it a man was sitting at a desk talking to a couple of other men, and when I pushed open the door, they all turned to look at me.

I don't know who was more surprised, me or the younger of my two stepbrothers, who I hadn't seen since I was a young child. For a moment, all I could think about were the many times when he'd offered me the choice of 'Football or a punch?' He was obviously as taken aback as I was, but he recovered more quickly and greeted me like a long-lost friend.

'Bloody hell, Peter! What are you doing here? Come on in.' He was grinning as he walked towards me with his hand outstretched and I found myself smiling back at him as I shook it. A few minutes later, we were sitting together in a corner of the caravan drinking mugs of coffee and reminiscing about the childhood we'd shared — or, at least, the few neutral, non-contentious aspects of it that were safe to discuss.

I told my stepbrother about the time I'd spent in the merchant navy and then the army and he told me about his job at SSL. It turned out he was a mechanic and was employed to help keep their fleet of vehicles running. By the time I'd finished my cup of coffee, I'd been employed by the company too, to work as a driver.

First, I had to learn how to handle the left-hand drive vehicles as well as the Fordson Major and Massey Ferguson tractors, which carried the water that was required to keep the drill bit cool during drilling. It was hard work and long hours — from dawn till dusk — but it was fun too, most of the time.

The company was searching for oil in the Gloucestershire countryside, using a process that involved drilling holes two hundred feet deep at numerous sites and lowering dynamite into them attached to wires with electronically detonated caps. Three small, round plugs — known as jugs — were then placed in the ground around each hole and connected by a length of half-inch electrical cable. When the explosives were detonated – from a Land Rover parked a safe distance away – a seismic reading was taken of the explosion, which was then analysed so that the possibility of there being oil or gas in the area could be assessed. It was another interesting job and I was fascinated by the process.

The water tankers I drove could hold a few thousand gallons of water, which was mixed with a brown powder to make 'mud' that was piped into a tin container and then fed down into the drill pipe to keep the drill bit cool and to bring up rock and limestone debris to clear the drill hole.

The farmers on whose land we were drilling were paid well, although I sometimes wondered if they regretted taking the money when they looked out across their fields on wet days and saw the muddy quagmire that had been churned up by the constant tracking of tyres.

The company used huge, fourteen-wheel International Harvesters, each of which had a telescopic rig on the bed and sixteen gears to pull them up steep hills and over difficult terrain. It was the surveyors' job to show the drillers where to drill, and once they'd decided on a location, they'd mark it by tying a red ribbon on the branch of a tree or inserting a stake into the ground. The driver of the vehicle would get as close to the marker as he could before elevating the rig from inside the cab, and then the two or three men working with him would make the drill ready. It was a complex process involving high-tech, complicated machinery and vehicles, which trundled across the countryside like massive, slow-moving robots from some futuristic film. It was dangerous work too.

One day, when we were working on a minor road between the villages of Guiting Power and Broadway, a surveyor had tied a red ribbon around a metal stake and hammered it into the ground without realizing that the spot he was marking was directly underneath some high power cables which ran across the road. Later that morning, the rig driver stopped bang on target and began to elevate the telescopic rig. When the rig made contact with the power lines, a huge surge of electric current shot down through the metal section and the vehicle was instantly engulfed in flames, killing all three of its occupants. It was all over in seconds. There was nothing anyone could have done to help those poor men. It was just one of those incredibly unfortunate – and mercifully rare – accidents, which I'm sure has remained with everyone else who witnessed it, as it has done with me.

Thankfully, not all the mishaps that occurred were tragic. One hot sunny Sunday, we were drilling on a grass verge beside the main road outside the village of Prestbury, a couple of miles from Cheltenham.

The hole had been drilled – in this instance, through blue clay – the dynamite had been lowered into it and the rig had moved on to its next location about a hundred yards along the road. When everything was in place and all the safety checks had been done, the detonation button was pressed. What we didn't know was that we'd struck an artesian well. When the dynamite exploded, the hole filled rapidly with dense blue water and as the pressure began to build, the water shot up into the air like a hundred-foot geyser. It was a spectacular sight.

In fact it wasn't uncommon to hit artesian wells, and there was a procedure to follow when it happened, which basically involved stopping all traffic in the immediate area until the water subsided and it was safe to proceed. On this occasion, however, no one had known about the well and so when the water exploded out of the hole like an aqueous rocket, it was too late to stop the young man who was riding his moped along the road en route to see his girlfriend and dressed immaculately in his Sunday best. When the deluge descended on him, he turned instantly blue, from the parting in his carefully combed hair to the toes of his well-polished shoes. He was very lucky not to have been blown off his bike – although I don't suppose 'lucky' was a word that entered his head at the time.

You couldn't help feeling sorry for the poor lad,

but it was impossible not to roar with laughter at the sight of him standing at the side of the road, bemused, soaked to the skin and looking as though he'd been dipped in a vat of indigo dye. When we were eventually able to control our amusement, we cleaned up his moped, mopped him down as much as we could – so that at least he wasn't soaking wet as well as bright blue – and the foreman wrote him a generous cheque to replace every single item of the clothing he was wearing. With the cheque in his hand, the young man at last began to see the funny side of what had happened, and even managed a smile when one of the drivers pointed out to him – amid gales of renewed laughter – that, thanks to the money he'd been given, he was now in the uncommon position of being simultaneously both happy and blue.

In addition to paying compensation to farmers for drilling on their land and to blue young men on mopeds, the company occasionally had to pay out more substantial amounts of money when other problems occurred. One such example arose when we were working in and around the village of Guiting Power.

We were drilling along a railway line that was one of the vast number of lines decommissioned in the 1960s as a result of the restructuring and drastic reduction of the railway network by Dr Richard

Beeching, chairman of the nationalized British Railways company. Our foreman, in his wisdom, had instructed us to drill all the holes required and blow them up together. Six holes had been drilled at intervals of about a hundred yards and when all the charges were detonated, it was as if the whole operation had been transposed into a scene from the Keystone Cops. As the shock waves spread out from the holes, every single greenhouse that had been standing at the end of almost every single garden backing on to the railway line collapsed like a pack of cards. After the initial explosive shattering of glass, there was almost total silence for a few seconds, and then a woman came running out of her house, shouting and brandishing a carving knife. As well as destroying her greenhouse, the shock waves had dislodged her entire, highly prized collection of commemorative and decorative plates from the Welsh dresser in her kitchen – where she'd been carving the Sunday roast with the knife she was now waving furiously in the air – and had sent them crashing to the ground. By the time the company had paid out to replace all the greenhouses and the woman's plate collection, the foreman had accepted the fact that there are some situations – such as during exploratory drilling for oil – in which time saving is not necessarily the prime consideration.

Working for SSL was a good job and I stayed with

the firm while they completed the work in the Cotswolds and then moved with them to Cheshire. To my knowledge, they never did find oil or gas in Cheshire and while we were there the company was disbanded and the drillers and drivers scattered to the four corners of the world to take up other jobs.

My stepbrother went to South Africa and we remained in intermittent and irregular contact for a few years. The last thing I heard was that he'd married and divorced several times and had ended up alone, propping up a bar in Cape Town. Clearly, his childhood experiences hadn't prepared him for a stable, happy adult life any more than mine had done.

Chapter 13

When the job with the oil company came to an end, it was time to start thinking about what I was going to do next. I hadn't reached any conclusions when one of the other lads said, 'I'm going home to Hampshire. There's a lot of work around where I live. In fact there's an old chap with a huge estate – I think he's a retired army major – who always seems to be looking for gamekeeper's assistants. It might be worth giving it a try. I could drop you off there on my way home if you want.'

I didn't have any better options, so I thanked him and took up his offer of a lift.

It was just starting to get dark when he dropped me by the gates at the end of a driveway that led to a large, square and very impressive-looking house. After he'd driven away, I stood there for a moment with my fingers curled tightly around the strap of my kitbag, trying to banish the unwanted memories of all the other driveways leading to all the other large houses that had featured in my childhood. Then I pulled myself together and walked through the open gates.

When I reached the house, I hesitated for a moment, unsure whether to go to the front door or round the back to the tradesmen's entrance. I decided confidence should be my watchword, and I lifted the heavy knocker on the solid oak front door and let it fall against the black, cast-iron head of a dog. I could hear the sound echoing as if through an empty hallway, and then the door was opened by a tall, slim man in his late sixties who was either the major himself or just happened to look like a caricature of everyone's idea of a typical retired army officer.

'Good evening, sir,' I said, in a tone I hoped was polite without sounding obsequious. 'I wondered if there might be a job for me on the estate. A friend of mine told me you might be in need of an assistant for your gamekeeper. I have to admit that it isn't my usual line of work, but I can turn my hand to almost anything.'

The man looked at me appraisingly for a moment and then took a step backwards, opened the door wide and said, in a pleasant, cultured voice, 'Well, I just might have a vacancy for a strong, fit young man like you. Why don't you come in and we'll discuss it.'

As I walked past him into the house, the thought crossed my mind that it wouldn't have been a good moment to light a match – you could have bottled the whisky fumes on his breath and sold them to homesick Scotsmen abroad.

The room he showed me into was impressive: the large rug in its centre was worn but expensive looking; there was a brown-leather armchair on either side of the fireplace and a beautiful white marble-top table on which stood a heavy bronze statue of a man with a shotgun in his hands and a dog at his feet.

We sat in the leather chairs while the major asked me questions about myself and about the work I'd been doing, and when he offered me the job of assistant gamekeeper and chauffeur, I accepted it immediately.

'Jolly good,' he said, smiling at me warmly and standing up to shake my hand. 'Well, as you're carrying everything you need in your kitbag, why don't you start in the morning? I'll show you to your room.'

After I'd dropped my bag on the floor of a small but comfortable-looking bedroom, he took me down to the kitchen where he introduced me to a man called Robert who made me a sandwich and a cup of tea.

It was good to sleep in a soft, warm bed again after so many nights in a caravan bunk, and I woke up the next morning feeling relaxed and optimistic. After I'd eaten an excellent breakfast, Robert took me out to meet the head gamekeeper, who was a man in his late forties called Tom.

Since discovering poetry at school and realizing

that learning can be fun, I've always loved gaining new knowledge, and learning how to rear and look after pheasants was no exception. The only part of my new duties I didn't like – and didn't ever do – was shooting the crows and squirrels that stole the food put out for the young pheasants and the cocks that roamed the fields and woods. What was even more of an anathema to me was the major's insistence that the heads and feet of the dead animals must be tied to the fences around the pheasant pens as a warning to other would-be predators and food thieves.

After a childhood that had involved many nights sleeping in dens and barns and wandering the countryside on my own, it was an environment I felt comfortable in, and I loved working outside. I'd been at the estate for several weeks and was doing routine maintenance work on some of the pheasant pens one morning when the gamekeeper came and stood beside me. At first, he didn't say anything; he just watched me. But when I stood up to stretch my back, he told me, 'You're a quick learner. I'm pleased with the way you're carrying out your duties.'

'Thanks,' I said, not looking at him directly so that he wouldn't see how pleased I was by what he'd said. 'I do my best.'

'There's just one problem,' he added. 'You're not shooting any crows or squirrels. The major must know about it, so I don't understand why he hasn't said anything to me. Has he mentioned it to you?'

'No,' I answered. 'I don't know why either.' The truth was I'd been hoping the major hadn't noticed, although that was unlikely in view of the satisfaction with which he often counted all the pathetic little bits of corpses tied to the fences around the pens. Even the fact that he seemed to like me didn't explain why he hadn't yet insisted on my doing the job the way he wanted it to be done.

I worked seven days a week, although there was no strict regime and the hours were mostly flexible, except in the evenings. Every afternoon at about four o'clock, I'd drive the old Land Rover back to the house, where I'd have a wash and something to eat. Robert had left a few days after I'd arrived and the job of cook had been taken over by a very nice woman who lived out, in a nearby village. I was told I could cook for myself whenever I wanted to do so, but I didn't often have to, because the new cook left good meals for me in the Aga.

At about seven thirty every night, I'd swap the Land Rover for the major's Austin Westminster and drive him to one or other of the two pubs in the village. Having dropped him there, I'd drive back to the house and await a phone call from the landlord to inform me that the pub was about to shut and my, by then well-oiled, employer was ready to be picked up. After I'd driven the major home from the pub, managed to manoeuvre him safely through the front door of the house and gone back outside again to put the car away, I'd let myself in through the back door and go upstairs to bed.

I'd learned many things during a turbulent childhood, among them was never to sit with my back to a door and always to lock the door of my bedroom. They are compulsions that remain with me to this day. The house I live in with my wife is like a fortress, with sturdy, high-quality locks – both visible and concealed – on all the doors, including the one in the high fence that surrounds the garden. There are many legacies of an unhappy, violent childhood, and a deep-rooted fear of someone creeping up on me is one of mine. So I was instantly alert when I was woken up at around midnight one Saturday night not long after the gamekeeper had spoken to me by the sound of someone turning the handle on my bedroom door.

I sat up in bed and listened. There it was again. It was too dark for me to be able to see the door handle and I didn't want to switch on the lamp by the bed, but the sound was unmistakable. Someone tapped on the door and I felt the damp heat of sweat on my back. For a moment, the house was silent and then the tapping turned to loud knocking and the major shouted, in a slurred, querulous voice, 'Let me in! Open the door!'

My fingernails were digging into the palms of my clenched fists and I had to swallow several times to try to force the panic back down inside me. Then the major's tone changed to drunken coaxing and he rattled the handle and called through the locked door, 'Let me in, Peter. I've got something I want to show you.'

At that moment, I wouldn't have opened my bedroom door if the house had been on fire, and eventually he gave up, leaving me to lie awake in my bed until the morning remembering the worst night of all the terrible nights of my childhood.

I haven't ever forgotten a single detail of the night I spent in a hotel room in Oxford. I've just never been able to bring myself to talk about it before. And although I was no longer a child and could easily have protected myself when the major knocked on my door in the middle of the night, the memory overwhelmed me and upset me so much that as he was stumbling back to his room, my heart was still racing.

I was fourteen years old when the master at the children's home called me into his office and told me I'd been chosen to have a special treat: I was to go to Oxford the following day to attend an ordination service at a church there. The man who'd be taking me was a local businessman and very actively involved with the village church we went to every Sunday. I didn't know where Oxford was, and I didn't have any real understanding of what was involved in an ordination service. It doesn't sound like much of a treat, I know, but any outing was exciting, and I felt very proud to have been picked.

'It's an honour,' the master added gravely. 'So make sure you behave yourself, do everything you're told to do without any argument, and don't let us – or yourself – down.'

'I won't, I promise,' I assured him, immediately anxious in case he should have second thoughts and change his mind.

The next morning, the sun was shining in a brilliant blue sky and I was up, washed and dressed in my Sunday best before anyone else. My stomach was so full of butterflies there was little room left in it for food, but I forced myself to eat some breakfast, just in case lunch was a long time coming. I could tell that some of the other boys were jealous, and I couldn't stop myself from savouring the moment and elaborating on the few details I'd been given by the master.

'We're going to see a maze after the service,' I told anyone who was listening at breakfast. 'It's the biggest and best maze in the whole country.' It was true that the master had said I might visit a maze, if there was time and if I behaved myself appropriately, but I had no basis for claiming that it was the biggest and best. 'And we might stay overnight in a hotel,' I added triumphantly; at that time in my life, I hadn't ever stayed in a hotel before.

As we were filing out of the dining room, I was called out of line and told that Mr Stephens had arrived in his car to collect me. There were lots of things I pretended not to care about – living in a children's home, it wasn't a good idea to wear your heart on your sleeve, or even to show that you had a heart at all – but I didn't bother with pretence on that occasion. I almost ran out of the front door and down the steps to the car.

Mr Stephens greeted me with a smile and said cheerfully, 'Well, now, Peter. Off we go, eh?' He got back in behind the wheel of his large, expensive car, and as I slid on to the leather seat beside him, I was unable to suppress a grin. The engine had just purred into life when he leaned across in front of me, opened the glove compartment and handed me a bag of sweets, saying, 'I almost forgot. These are for you.'

Excitement made me garrulous and as we sped through the countryside, past fields and farm buildings, I chatted away happily, answering the questions Mr Stephens asked me and munching on the sweets he'd given me. I didn't have any idea at all how far it was to Oxford and when I asked if we were nearly there, he smiled and patted my knee as he replied, 'Not far now. I'm keen to get there too.'

I knew it was Oxford as soon as we arrived – the master had been right about the magnificent old buildings. Mr Stephens parked the car and then put his hand on my arm to steer me across the road to the church. The pews were hard and the service was long and boring, but sitting through it was a small price to pay for a day out and the possibility of spending the night in a hotel. At last the ordination was over and as we left the dark church, I tried to look suitably serious as I assured Mr Stephens in answer to his questions that it was, indeed, an impressive building and that the ordination service had been very interesting.

'Well, what would you say to something to eat and perhaps an ice cream before we have a look at this famous maze?' he asked, dropping his arm casually on to my shoulders as we walked down the road towards the car.

I think the maze must have been at Blenheim Palace, and it was even better than I'd imagined it would be. After lunch in a cafe, while Mr Stephens sat and drank a cup of tea, I ran around in the sunshine with all the other children who were playing there and had the time of my life. I still couldn't believe I'd been lucky enough to be the one who'd been chosen to have such a wonderful treat. I'd been playing for some time when I saw Mr Stephens stand up and start to scan the group of laughing children who were chasing each other across the grass. I knew he was looking for me and I ran towards him.

'Well, I think we'd better be going, don't you?' he said, nodding as if I'd already agreed with him.

I put my hands behind my back and crossed my fingers. I'd already had a really good day out, so I knew it was greedy to hope for more. But I couldn't help it: not only would staying in a hotel be the most exciting thing that had ever happened to me, I could only imagine how envious it would make all the other children at the home. So when Mr Stephens said, 'I expect you'll soon be hungry again, and we need to get to the hotel in time for you to have a wash before we eat,' I couldn't suppress a whoop of delight. And when I ran back to say goodbye to the children I'd been playing with, I couldn't resist telling them proudly, 'I have to go now. Mister . . . my uncle's taking me to stay the night in a hotel.'

Mr Stephens parked the car in the hotel car park and I lifted my small overnight bag off the back seat before following him up the steps of a large stone building whose mullioned windows were lit by the glow of a warm yellow light. The door of the hotel was opened for us by a doorman wearing a crimson, gold-buttoned uniform, and after Mr Stephens had checked in at the polished mahogany reception desk, we went up in the lift to a large twin-bedded room with its *own* bathroom.

A few minutes later, after a quick wash, we were back in the lift again – this time on our way down to the restaurant on the first floor, where the tables were covered with thick white tablecloths, the cutlery was silver and the butter was shaped into small, ridged curls. The waiter called me 'sir', Mr Stephens drank wine and laughed loudly when I made a joke, and by the end of the meal I thought I knew what it must feel like to win the football pools.

Back in our room after supper, I washed my hands and face yet again, cleaned my teeth, put on my pyjamas and took a flying leap on to my bed. Mr Stephens did the same shortly afterwards – with the exception of jumping on to his bed – and while he read his book in the lamplight, I fell into a deep, untroubled sleep.

When I woke up, it was pitch dark and for a moment I couldn't think where I was. It felt as if there was something heavy on my bed and then I heard a voice whisper, 'Are you awake?' That's when I remembered I was in a hotel room in Oxford, and I realized it must be Mr Stephens, churchman, businessman and benefactor to deprived and troubled children, who was sitting on my bed and talking to me.

I'd been lying on my stomach and, as I began to sit up, a hand pushed me back down again and I felt fingers touching my hair.

'It's all right.' Mr Stephens' voice was low and strangely muffled. 'You just lie there quietly and be a good boy. I'm going to make a man of you tonight.'

I was too frightened and shocked by what he did to me to make any sound at all. I barely breathed, and at one point I thought I was going to suffocate and die, which couldn't have been any worse than enduring what was happening.

You feel guilty after something like that, as if it was your fault rather than the fault of the person who abused you. At fourteen, I was still very young for my age and I didn't really understand what had been done to me. What I had learned, through bitter experience, was that it was usually best to do what adults told me to do, because railing against them always landed me in trouble. Perhaps that was partly why I didn't shout and struggle and fight Mr Stephens off – that and the facts that he was strong, he was hurting me and I was in a state of shock.

When it was all over, he went back to his bed and I turned on to my back, felt for the covers that were in a tangled heap on the floor and pulled them up to my neck. I didn't sleep again that night and as soon as it was light, I got up, got dressed, packed my few belongings into my case and sat on my bed, waiting for Mr Stephens to wake up and return me to the safety of the children's home.

I didn't tell anyone what had happened – what would I have said, when I didn't really understand what it was myself? And, in any case, I knew from experience that all complaining got you was punishment for telling lies.

After that day, a few other boys had special treats and went on outings with Mr Stephens and sometimes, when they came back to the home, I'd see them looking at me with a questioning sort of expression on their faces. They'd always turn away quickly if I caught their eye, and they'd make some comment to no one in particular to show how tough they were and that they weren't the sort of boy to stand any nonsense or ever have to ask anyone else for help. And although I never said anything, I knew how they felt.

I've never been back to Oxford since that day, and I've carried the terrible burden of that abuse for fifty-six years. It brings tears to my eyes and pain to my heart even now when I hear about people who suffered sexual abuse as children and were too frightened to tell anyone about it, or, worse, were ignored when they did. No punishment is too severe for someone who's been responsible for destroying the life of a child in that way.

When the major knocked on my door in the middle

of the night all those years later, it brought back memories I didn't ever want to think about. This time though, I wasn't a defenceless, frightened boy who'd had it drummed into his head for the previous twelve years that the one thing above all others that was guaranteed to get you into trouble was not doing what adults told you to do. *I* was an adult, an ex-sailor and an ex-soldier, and I knew how to defend myself. Despite that, however, when the major came knocking, I was instantly transformed into a damaged, scared child again. It felt as if a trust had been broken, and I knew I couldn't stay there any longer.

The next day, I told Tom what had happened the previous night. He just shrugged and gave me a strange look as he said, 'I thought you knew. I thought everyone knew. You can't keep that sort of thing quiet in a small community like this. I mean, it's obvious really, isn't it?'

It hadn't been 'obvious' to me.

I gave my week's notice to Tom, who informed the major that I was leaving, and then I caught a train from Southampton to the small town in the Cotswolds that was the only place I'd ever really thought of as home.

Chapter 14

By the end of my first day back in Gloucestershire, I'd rented and moved into a bedsit, and the next morning I found work as a driver for a firm of hauliers. I didn't last very long in that job – I didn't have the stomach or the heart for delivering animals to the slaughterhouse, which was what the work sometimes entailed. But it was the 1960s and work was plentiful, and within a day of leaving there, I got a job in a local foundry. Then I got itchy feet again and moved on to work as a driving instructor, then in engineering, then delivering coaches to Basel in Switzerland, then working as a bus driver for the East Kent Bus Service in Folkestone . . .

Although I enjoyed almost every job I did, earned good money and learned many new skills, I didn't seem to be able to settle to anything. I'd bought myself a second-hand Humber Hawk, which was my pride and joy, and when the wife of a friend asked me one day if I'd drive her to Cheshire, I agreed. She wanted to visit a friend of hers – a widow with two young daughters – who'd just come out of hospital after having traction for a slipped disc.

It's funny how a chain of events that can dramatically alter the course of your life can start with something as simple as doing a favour for a friend.

We set out early on a Saturday morning in September 1969 and arrived at a terraced house in Cheadle Heath, a suburb of Stockport, at around nine thirty in the morning. When my friend knocked on the door, it was opened by a woman I recognized immediately. I didn't know her – I hadn't ever seen her before; but when I looked into her face as she stood there on the doorstep of her house that morning, it was like releasing a long-held breath. I knew I'd found the thing I'd been searching for all my life without ever having been aware that's what I was doing.

Anne made us cups of tea and introduced me to her daughters, Martine and Michelle, and I sat in total contentment listening to the two women talking about past times in their lives and about what they hoped the future might hold for them.

What makes two people fall in love? Is it chemistry? Biology? Are there such things as soul mates and kindred spirits? No one knows the answers to those questions. Love might just as well be controlled after all by Cupid and his arrows. What's even more amazing than the fact of my falling in love that day is that when I drove a friend to Stockport and found the woman of my dreams, she fell in love with me too.

Anne and I were married less than four months after we'd first set eyes on each other, and at last I felt I'd come home and could really start to live my life.

Somehow – I can't remember how; perhaps I told them myself – my brother and sisters found out about my plans to marry and for a while the telephone seemed to ring constantly as they all phoned me up to advise me against it. Their initial opposition was nothing, however, compared to their uniformly hysterical response to being told that Anne was a widow with two young daughters. I had no idea why they were so opposed to the prospect of our pending marriage, and even less interest in their opinions.

With the exception of the day when my brother had threatened to tell the police if my father and Flossie continued to treat me the way they were doing, and the time he'd pushed my head down amongst the vegetables in the garden to hide me when my father ran amok with a hatchet, none of my siblings had ever lifted a finger to help me in twenty-seven years. The little contact I'd had with them had been mostly restricted to being invited to the house of one or other of my sisters whenever they wanted to borrow some money. At least, 'borrow' is what they liked to call it, whereas I knew as well as they did that I'd never see a single penny of it again.

Anne and I didn't receive a card or even a piece of

paper with a hastily scribbled message of goodwill from any member of my family when we got married. Anne couldn't understand their attitude and for years blamed herself for the rift between us. But it wasn't her fault at all. She hadn't any experience of the sort of spiteful nastiness my family was capable of, and so she couldn't understand that, in fact, it was a very good thing we didn't have any contact with them, because the truth was that wherever they went, they took with them nothing but trouble.

Over the years, before I met Anne, I'd sometimes get depressed and think about killing Flossie and my father – not because of what they'd done to me, but because of the unhappiness I believed they'd caused my mother and because of their apparently total indifference to her death. It seems a bizarre notion when I think about it now, but it was real enough at the time, and I don't know what might have happened if I hadn't met and fallen in love with Anne when I did.

Whatever happens to us – whatever cruelty and hardships we encounter – we're all responsible for our own actions and for how we live our lives. It's easy to blame other people, but I had a choice about what I did, just as Flossie and my father had a choice about the way they behaved. By harming them, I'd have done far more harm to myself. So I had many reasons to be thankful that I met Anne and that I'd chosen every path I'd ever chosen in my life that led me eventually to her house on that day in September.

By marrying Anne I was making a new start and taking the first step towards creating the future I'd always wanted. Drawing a line under the unhappiness of my childhood, I relegated it firmly and irrevocably to the past – and the past is where my family belonged too.

We began our married life in Anne's house in Stockport, where I got a job at the Bredbury steel-rolling mill. I've had more than sixty jobs during my working lifetime – I never did find a cure for those itchy feet – but that was the hardest one of all. So, one Saturday in June, when we'd been married for five months, we loaded the girls into the car and drove to Gloucestershire to look for a new home. By the end of the day, we'd put down a fifty-pound deposit on a brand new two-bedroom bungalow and when we moved in six weeks later, I started a well-paid, very interesting job working for a firm that developed electric cars and scooters for disabled people.

Sometimes, when we were all sitting together at the dinner table eating our evening meal or the girls had their heads bent over their homework while Anne and I did tasks around the house, I'd look at them and feel tears of wonder and gratitude pricking my eyes. Before I was married, I'd had friends, done some jobs I'd enjoyed, and seen more of the world than I'd ever thought I'd see. But I hadn't had anything that was really *mine*, and I'd known I was lacking the most important thing of all: someone who cared deeply about me. And then, within the space of just nine months, I'd gone from having nothing to having everything I'd ever wanted: I had a family, and I loved them with a fierce, protective passion.

One day, when the girls had settled into their new schools and our lives had become comfortable and contented, I asked Anne what she thought about my adopting Martine and Michelle. For some reason, I'd been thinking about what would happen if Anne and I were both to die at the same time – in a car accident, for example – and the thought that my share of everything we owned together might go, not to the girls, but to my father, if he was still alive, and/or to my siblings, filled me with an almost physical sense of distress.

Anne agreed immediately to put my suggestion to Martine and Michelle and later that day we explained it to them in a way they could understand.

Martine was twelve at the time and, having listened to what we were telling her, she declined to be adopted. I was disappointed, but I could appreciate her reasons: it was less than four years since she'd lost her father and she wasn't ready to take what she saw as a very big step, despite being able to see its value in practical terms.

Michelle, who was just eight, accepted readily, however. Perhaps her memories of her father were already more indistinct than those of her sister, so maybe what was most important to her was the need to feel she belonged. If so, it was a feeling with which I could empathize only too well. I went through the process of legally adopting Michelle, but, adopted or otherwise, it didn't make any difference to the way I felt about the girls: to me, they were both my daughters and I loved them and wanted to do my best for them.

Martine had a mind of her own and often didn't choose the path her mother, or I, would have chosen for her, which is what happened when she was six-teen and she and her boyfriend decided they wanted to get married. To say that Anne and I weren't over the moon about it would be an understatement, but in the end we bowed to Martine's insistence and the marriage went ahead.

In May 1982, when Martine suffered an aneurysm in her head, the oldest of her three sons was just seven. On the twenty-second of that month, her husband gave his permission for her life-support machine to be turned off. It was a terrible day for all of us.

After Martine's death, her husband wasn't short of offers of help to bring up their three sons, but he chose to put them in care. It was a decision that broke Anne's heart for a second time. I was devastated too. In reality, however, I knew it wasn't the worst decision he could have made. I'd learned from my own experiences that although being brought up in a children's home isn't something you'd wish for any child – let alone a child that's part of your own family – it's sometimes the lesser of two evils.

It was almost two years after Martine's death, when I was working as a maintenance fitter on fork-lift trucks at a large animal feeds mill, that I received a phone call from Flossie. At first, I couldn't work out who it was. It was as if my mind had blocked her out completely and when she said, 'It's your step-mother. It's Flossie,' I struggled to get a mental picture of the woman on the other end of the telephone line. She must have realized I was drawing a blank – or perhaps she thought I was pretending – because she sounded irritable when she told me, 'Your father's very ill. You'd better come.'

The words, 'I don't care; I don't even want to know,' had already travelled from my brain to my mouth and I only just managed to stop myself saying them out loud. Instead, I told Flossie that Anne and I would visit him that evening.

When we arrived at the bungalow in Cheltenham,

we were shown into what used to be my bedroom when I had my first, brief, job as an apprentice blacksmith. Flossie looked strained and tired, but I couldn't find it in my heart to feel sorry for her. In fact, I didn't feel anything for her at all, not even the hatred I thought I'd feel at the sight of her and at the memory of the misery she created for me from the time when I was two years old.

My father looked as ill as he was. As I stood by his bed with my wife, he kept apologizing, telling me how sorry he was for everything that had happened and for the way he'd treated me when I was a child. Generally I'm a soft-hearted person, troubled by other people's misfortunes and reduced to tears by stories of unkindness to children and animals. But again I felt nothing as I looked down at my father lying there on his deathbed.

'Don't worry about it,' I told him, not wanting to hear the words he was saying at last, now that it was far too late for them to have any meaning at all. 'Don't worry. It doesn't matter any more.'

We didn't stay very long, and after I'd said goodbye, I grasped the hand that Anne held out to me and left my father's house for the last time.

Three days after that visit, I was at work when I was called to the office and told, 'There's someone here to see you.' I think I knew the reason for the summons, but I wasn't prepared to see the bearer of the news – my half-sister, the little queen – standing in the office at my place of work.

'He's dead,' she wailed as soon as I walked into the room. 'Our father's dead.' Then she broke down and sobbed like a child.

I know she was genuinely upset – although we'd shared a childhood in terms of time, her experiences couldn't have been more different from mine. I don't know what the people in the office thought when I made no attempt to comfort her.

I was still standing at a distance from her, near the door, when I told her, 'Anne and I will come to the funeral.' Then I left her in the office and went back to work.

When Martine died, I'd known her for just twelve years, but I'd loved her as a daughter. For a long time after her death, I'd be doing something in the house or at work when grief would suddenly make my heart lurch, as if an invisible hand had reached into my chest and punched it. The news of my father's death, however, left me completely cold. They say there's a special part of your heart reserved for the love of your parents. If that's the case, the part where love for my father should have resided had atrophied and turned to stone a long time ago. It was the same when my eldest sister died some years later: I felt nothing. Although perhaps that wasn't quite the same, because despite having no reason to like her, I'd never hated her.

In the end, I didn't go to my father's funeral service. I just went with my brother to the chapel of rest in Cheltenham, where we behaved in the very inappropriate but cathartic way I described at the start of my story. That was the last time I ever saw my brother. We spoke on the telephone a few times, but there wasn't much to say, because we had nothing in common except for the fact that we'd had the same diabolical father and stepmother, which was something we both wanted to forget.

By some quirk of fate – or perhaps deliberately, I'll never know – shortly after my father's death, Flossie bought a house on the estate where Anne and I were living. We avoided her and she soon moved again, this time to live near her eldest son. We didn't hear anything more about her until she died – in a nursing home – and her son divided up what was left of her money among us all. I received five hundred pounds, which I gave to Michelle. I wouldn't have kept a penny of it: I'd only ever wanted one thing from Flossie, and by that time it was sixty years too late.

After I married Anne, the hatred I used to feel for my stepmother and father simply died. Sometimes, I'd try to resurrect it by thinking about the worst things they'd done to me when I was a child, but for some reason it didn't work. When I had a family of my own, Flossie and Harold didn't seem to matter any more and I realized that if I *did* hate them, the hatred would be like a cancer growing inside me, spreading its poison over all the good things in my life, and in the end I'd be the one who suffered as a result of it.

It was my daughter, Michelle, who prompted me to tell my life story. She was a lovely child who grew up to be a wonderful woman. She works in a care home and was on a training course when she was asked to relate brief details of the life story of one of her parents. 'Mum's life story is normal,' she told me. 'So I need to know yours.' And that's how I came to write it all down. I could never have told my story without the support of my wife and daughter, and it would still be whirling around in my head like a destructive secret.

I was sixty-nine years old when I finally let it go. Of course, I'll never forget what happened in my childhood, but at least I've now accepted the fact that it wasn't my fault. I didn't do anything to deserve the treatment I received at the hands of my own father and his new wife. No two-year-old child is wilfully, perversely naughty, and no child is innately unlovable. Sadly, knowing that and believing it about yourself can be two very different things.

You never get over a desperately unhappy child-hood and you never know when a memory from the past is going to steal the wind from your sails. Some people refer to those unwanted memories as flash-backs. Whatever you call them, I've learned over the years to avoid certain triggers, such as reading articles in the newspaper or listening to news reports about terrible things that have been done to children. Writing this book has helped too, because it has enabled me to capture the past and contain it, so that I can focus on the present and on the future.

Thirty years ago, I started writing poems for children, some of which were used by the BBC on *Poetry Corner* for schools, and some appeared in pub-lished anthologies. I write poems for grown-ups now – for myself – as a way of expressing emotions that are otherwise difficult, if not impossible, to deal with.

After more than forty years of marriage, Anne is still the centre of my world, Michelle is a mother with children of her own, and I'm a proud and doting husband, father and grandfather. The house where Flossie used to live before my mother died was pulled down many years ago and the land where it once stood is now a play area and picnic site for children with special needs. Sometimes out of evil comes good.

I still never feel completely safe, despite all the

locks and security devices I've installed in the house and garden. And I never sit with my back to a door. Now though, they're just old habits that I've accepted I'll never break. I know there's nothing I really need to be afraid of.

Something else that's irrational but irrevocable is the wish that, although I was only two years old when my mother died, I'd been able to do something to help her. I don't know what she would have wished for me – certainly not the childhood I had. Perhaps she'd have wanted me to know what it was like to love and be loved. If that's the case, she can rest in peace.

A Good Boy

I woke before the morning, I was happy all the day,
I never said an ugly word, but smiled and stuck to play

And now at last the sun is going down behind the
    wood,
And I am very happy, for I know that I've been good.

My bed is waiting cool and fresh, with linen smooth
    and fair,
And I must be off to sleepsin-by, and not forget my
    prayer.

I know that, till to-morrow I shall see the sun arise,
No ugly dream shall fright my mind, no ugly sight my
    eyes.

But slumber hold me tightly till I waken in the dawn,
And hear the thrushes singing in the lilacs round the
    lawn.

Robert Louis Stevenson

The Brook

I come from haunts of coot and hern,
I make a sudden sally
And sparkle out among the fern,
To bicker down a valley.

By thirty hills I hurry down,
Or slip between the ridges,
By twenty thorpes, a little town,
And half a hundred bridges.

Till last by Philip's farm I flow
To join the brimming river,
For men may come and men may go,
But I go on for ever.

I chatter over stony ways,
In little sharps and trebles,
I bubble into eddying bays,
I babble on the pebbles.

With many a curve my banks I fret
By many a field and fallow,
And many a fairy foreland set
With willow-weed and mallow.

I chatter, chatter, as I flow
To join the brimming river,
For men may come and men may go,
But I go on for ever.

I wind about, and in and out,
With here a blossom sailing,
And here and there a lusty trout,
And here and there a grayling,

And here and there a foamy flake
Upon me, as I travel
With many a silvery waterbreak
Above the golden gravel,

And draw them all along, and flow
To join the brimming river,
For men may come and men may go,
But I go on for ever.

I steal by lawns and grassy plots,
I slide by hazel covers;
I move the sweet forget-me-nots
That grow for happy lovers.

I slip, I slide, I gloom, I glance,
Among my skimming swallows;
I make the netted sunbeam dance
Against my sandy shallows.

I murmur under moon and stars
In brambly wildernesses;
I linger by my shingly bars;
I loiter round my cresses;

And out again I curve and flow
To join the brimming river,
For men may come and men may go,
But I go on for ever.

Alfred Lord Tennyson

SOPHIE YOUNG

PLEASE WILL SOMEONE HELP ME?

This family moved into the area last month . . . health visitor not available but appears that there was some hearsay that there was child abuse. Last week on Wednesday morning seen by Doctor - he saw on child's buttocks very deep bruising by mark of hand. When questioned, Mrs Gilmore denied hitting the child. Doctor's receptionist said there is a lot of gossip.
Social work report 4325G/Sophie Gilmore

Sophie Young (nee Gilmore) was born into a dysfunctional family, with a violent mother and father. Sophie was routinely neglected and harmed, starved and left to fend for herself. Social workers were often involved but, despite numerous visits and extensive reports, nothing was ever done.

When Sophie was six, her life took another horrible turn: her adored grandfather began to sexually abuse her.

With full access to her social work files, Sophie tells her heartbreaking story, showing how those who are meant to help children can be blind to the reality of their lives; but how, ultimately, love conquers all.

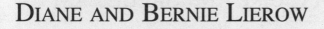

DIANE AND BERNIE LIEROW

DANI'S STORY

Neglected beyond belief, rescued by love . . .

Dani was so severely neglected by her birth mother that she grew up knowing only squalor. She never went to school or the doctor, and rarely glimpsed sunlight. Desperately malnourished, she couldn't talk and had never been toilet-trained. The social worker who took her into care had never heard of a case so horrific. The doctors believed Dani would never recover from such a terrible start in life.

Then she met the Lierows - a unique, blended family who were seeking to adopt a child. Despite being warned that she was way beyond hope of a normal life, they were instantly drawn to her and sensed a bright light behind her pale complexion. When they finally adopted her, they showered Dani with so much affection and encouragement that she came to life for the first time. Proving all the experts wrong, Dani would go on to open up and express herself in a way that no-one could have expected.

Dani's remarkable and heartwarming story is a testament of the power of kindness to overcome even the most seemingly insurmountable challenges.

TONI MAGUIRE AND SALLY EAST

DON'T YOU LOVE YOUR DADDY?

Every child needs to be loved. But Sally's desire to be told she was special came at a price no child should have to pay. She was only three years old when she felt her Daddy's large hands moving under her skirt when she sat on his knee.

Her beloved mother suspected that something was wrong, but instead of tackling her husband, she took refuge in the bottle. She died when Sally was just six. There had been no goodbyes, no warnings, and for many years, no closure.

With no other adult in the home, Sally's father was free to indulge in his urge to molest his daughter . . .

This is the harrowing true story of an innocent little girl who grew up with unbearable memories of horrendous mental and physical abuse.

Toni Maguire is the bestselling author of *Don't Tell Mummy*, *When Daddy Comes Home*, *Helpless* and *Nobody Came*.

Toni Maguire and Jackie Holmes

CAN'T ANYONE HELP ME?

Abused, unloved and alone: the true story of a little girl with a terrible secret

Jackie was an unwanted child. So unwanted that her mother regularly left Jackie at her uncle's house. Which was when the nightmare started. For when his wife went out, her uncle's friends came round. He had a Special Room. In it Jackie was tied up and molested, beaten, burnt by cigarettes and urinated on. Sometimes other children were brought along. Jackie got to know the Special Room intimately.

Jackie could never bring herself to tell her mother. She ended up in a home for disturbed children. She ran away, and a life of homelessness, drugs, prostitution and psychiatric wards followed.

Eventually, Jackie sought help. But could she turn her life around? Would her evil uncle and his Special Room haunt her forever?

Can't Anyone Help Me? is the inspirational story of struggle and survival against all odds as one young woman attempts to put her torturous past behind her and make a future for herself.

He just wanted a decent book to read ...

Not too much to ask, is it? It was in 1935 when Allen Lane, Managing Director of Bodley Head Publishers, stood on a platform at Exeter railway station looking for something good to read on his journey back to London. His choice was limited to popular magazines and poor-quality paperbacks – the same choice faced every day by the vast majority of readers, few of whom could afford hardbacks. Lane's disappointment and subsequent anger at the range of books generally available led him to found a company – and change the world.

'We believed in the existence in this country of a vast reading public for intelligent books at a low price, and staked everything on it'
Sir Allen Lane, 1902–1970, founder of Penguin Books

The quality paperback had arrived – and not just in bookshops. Lane was adamant that his Penguins should appear in chain stores and tobacconists, and should cost no more than a packet of cigarettes.

Reading habits (and cigarette prices) have changed since 1935, but Penguin still believes in publishing the best books for everybody to enjoy. We still believe that good design costs no more than bad design, and we still believe that quality books published passionately and responsibly make the world a better place.

So wherever you see the little bird – whether it's on a piece of prize-winning literary fiction or a celebrity autobiography, political tour de force or historical masterpiece, a serial-killer thriller, reference book, world classic or a piece of pure escapism – you can bet that it represents the very best that the genre has to offer.

Whatever you like to read – trust Penguin.